The Peer Family in North America

V. 5 Stephen Peer & His Wife Lydia Skinner and their Descendants to 3 Generations

by Lorine McGinnis Schulze

ISBN: 978-1-987938-03-6
Copyright 2016
All rights reserved
Publisher Olive Tree Genealogy

Cover Image Credit: Library and Archives Canada, Acc. No. 1990-586-3
Maps by Brian L. Massey

Introduction

My grandmother Olive McGinnis was a Peer by birth. My website Olive Tree Genealogy is named in her honour. My father, one of her six sons, knew very little of his ancestry. He often spoke about wanting to know more and his early death at age 47 prompted me to find the answers he had so long sought.

Researching the Peer families in North America has been a labour of love. In the last 30 years I have accumulated a great deal of information and source documents. There are several ways I could have tackled the task of compiling these findings, and the findings that other descendants have kindly shared.

Publishing the findings as one book proved to be impossible. The size of it would have been overwhelming. The cost would have been prohibitive. Thus I decided to split what would have been a 1000 pages or more sized book into smaller separate volumes. Splitting the book into separate volumes has the added benefit of allowing descendants to purchase their direct family line at a greatly reduced cost rather than pay for one huge book with information that might not be of interest to them.

Volume 1 is the story of Jacob, his wife Anne and their known children. All descendants will need Volume 1, as it provides data and documentation for Jacob and Anne as well as details of their lives in New Jersey and Upper Canada (Ontario).

Each of Jacob and Anne's known children are listed in Volume 1, along with their spouses, birth years and locations and death years and locations when known. Subsequent volumes contain source documents, details, and a genealogy report of descendants for each of Jacob and Anne's children.

This book follows Jacob's son Stephen Peer & his wife Lydia Skinner. Inside are found genealogy records, letters, documents, photographs and genealogy reports to 3 generations.

Table of Contents

Stephen Peer and his wife Lydia Skinner

Stephen Peer was born circa 1780 New Jersey to Jacob & Anna Peer. His parents were Jacob and Ann Peer who are thoroughly discussed in Volume 1 of this series. He was killed at the Battle of Chippewa during the War of 1812, on 5 July 1814. He married Lydia Skinner who was baptised 13 August 1785 in New York to Haggai Skinner & Elizabeth Westbrook.

In his father Jacob's will of 1810 he is listed as *"my son Stephen Peer - 100 pounds currency of New York to be paid ..... after the decease of my wife Anne"*.

Stephen married Lydia Skinner, daughter of the Loyalist Haggai Skinner and wife Elizabeth Westbrook. Lydia received her Orders in Council on 16 Apr. 1809, and it is very possible that this is the year she married Stephen. They settled in the village of Stamford, in Stamford Township, Lincoln County in the Niagara area of Ontario, not far from his family.

On March 1, 1811, Lydia petitioned as the daughter of a Loyalist for lands from the Crown. In her petition she stated she was the daughter of Haggai Skinner and was married to Stephen Peer. She was recommended for a grant of 200 acres as the daughter of a Loyalist. A notation on the outside of her petition, states that Warrant A97 of 17 April 1811 was paid "by her husband". [1]

Stephen and Lydia's son Stephen was born in 1811 and shortly after, the War of 1812 started. Stephen enlisted in Captain Rowe's Company, 2nd Lincoln and became a noted marksman.

Stephen was killed during the War of 1812 in the Battle of Chippawa on 5 July 1814. He was a private in the 2nd Regiment of Lincoln Militia under the command of Thomas Dickson. His second son Edward was born almost one month after Stephen's death. In a letter, Dickson identifies his widow as Lydia Peer, with 2 children. [2]

> *"Stephen Peer was in Captain John Rowe's Company of the 2nd Lincolns. He "resided with his wife Lydia in a neat white frame house below the hill. [Christopher Buchner had settled on the large sand hill that overlooked the junction of the portage road and a side route known as Lundy's Lane.] Peer was a recent immigrant from the United States who had married into the numerous Skinner clan, a Loyalist family who farmed south of Buchner's place. He may have been somewhat relunctant to march ot Chippawa on 5 July as his wife was eight months pregnant with their second child. Among the dead were James Forsyth and Stephen Peer - the latter would never see his son, born twenty-six days later."* [3]

"Peer Street [in Stamford Village] takes its name from Stephen Peer, a noted rifleman of the 2nd Lincoln, who fell at Chippewa. The frame of his house, which ws riddled by balls during the Battle of Lundy's Lane, still does duty in two dwellings nearby. Peer Street leads to Polly Town." [4]

Stephen's will was probated 26 Sept. 1815. In it he spoke of his wife Lydia, his son Stephen and his brothers and sisters (unnamed)

In the Name of God Amen, the Eleventh of September in the Year of our Lord one Thousand Eight Hundred and Thirteen [consulted original will to read the date], I Stephen Peer of the Township of Stamford, County of Lincoln, District of Niagara, in the Province of Upper canada, being weak in body but of perfect [illegible] and [illegible]. Thanks be to God for the same and calling to mind [illegible] of my body and knowing [illegible] this is my last Will and Testament.

I give and recommend my soul into the hands of God [illegible] in a decent manner at the discretion of my Executors hoping [illegible] General resurrection to obtain everlasting happiness [illegible] of my [illegible - blessed?] Redeemer Jesus Christ. And as to [illegible] wordly estate if it pleased God to [illegible] in this life, I give [illegible] of the same in the manner and [illegible] following:

In the first place I give and bequeath to Lydia my beloved wife all my household furniture, of every denomination [illegible], one cow, all the other [illegible] to be sold to pay my just debts. She is likewise to remain on my farm I now dwell on [illegible] remains my widow, that is to say till my son Stephen comes of age, it is to be understood that if my effects [illegible portion][satisfy my just deamnds she is to pay the [illegible] creditors from the Produce of my farm, but if it should [illegible] that she should change her condition before my said son Steph [part cut off] should come of age, then the farm rents and profits [illegible section] my said son Stephen. Except twenty-five pounds [insert illegible] for [illegible] paid to her my said wife, Lydia during the term of her life and should so happen that if she my said wife [illegible] and likewise my son Stephen and [illegible sentence] all my land property to be sold and the profits equally [illegible] my brothers and sisters then surviving [illegible portion] for every just demand satisfied.

[illegible section] ordain my wife Lydia [illegible] and Lanty Shannon, Executors of this my last [illegible] and Testament. In witness whereof I have herewith [illegible] my hand and seal [illegible]

Signed Stephen Peer
Witnesses [illegible] DeWitt
John Misener

Lydia, widow of Stephen Peer, Private, War of 1812, received a pension in 1816 of 20 pounds. [5] Lydia & Stephen had one son and Lydia was 8 months pregnant when Stephen was killed in July 1814. His second son Edward was born in August 1814, one month after Stephen's death. His son Stephen named in father's will of 1813, and he was the child born 1811 as per the Widow's Pension Lists.

Also LDS Film 170143 No. (1805?)179 L 3 C7 Crowland Twp; No. 180 L172 Stamford Twp;No.181 Pt L143 Stamford; and No.182 L197 Stamford all deal with Stephen Peer of Stamford Twp, Blacksmith.

War of 1812 Claims for Losses

Canada, Loyalist Claims, 1776-1835 about Widow Peer
Name: Widow Peer
Residence Year: 1801 - 1835
Correspondence Date: 7 May 1824
Record Type: Account of Losses
Piece Description: Miscellaneous
see image

also 7 March 1825
see images in Documents Section

Canada, Loyalist Claims, 1776-1835 about Widow Peer
Name: Widow Peer
Residence Year: 1801 - 1835
Record Type: Account of Losses
Piece Description: Miscellaneous

Lydia Skinner Peer & John Barker

Lydia remarried in Niagara on 06 September 1818 to John Barker. [6]

I suggest that Lydia and John Barker had the following children:

* Julia
* Edgar
* Lydia

In Dunnville at the residence of the bride's brother-in-law (not named], on Thurs. 22nd ult., James Adams, of St. Louis, Mo., merchant, & Lydia, daughter of J. Barker, of Niagara. (Rev. A. Townley)

October 1853 Marriage Records in Ontario Marriage Notices [1830-1856]

Stephen Peer & Ann Forster

Stephen's birth was in August 1811 in Stamford. He bought property in Markham Twp in 1836. He was listed "of Stamford in Lincoln County, Niagara District". [Source: Tanya Blundell]

Brown's Toronto City & Home District Directory 1846-1847: Stephen Peer, Lot 12, Conc. 7, Markham

Roswell's [Rowsell's?] City of Toronto & County of York Directory, 1850-1851: Stephen Peer, Lot v. 12 Conc 7 Markham

Edward Pears, L35 Conc 1 Markham

Markham, 1793-1900 /by Committee for the History of Markham Township. Markham Historical Society, c1979. # Subjects Markham (Ont. : Township) -- History. ISBN: 0969090005 Description: viii, 373 p. : ill.
Notes: Includes index. Additional Authors: Champion, Isabel. Markham Historical Society (Ont.). Page 259:

"Another product of Markham Village was bells. The enterprise was started by Stephen PEER in a foundry on the south-east corner of the Robinson millpond. Levi Jones and Company operated the
bell foundry from 1860 on followed by the Peter GEE family. Prices were as follows:
15" diameter bell yoke and crank- $ 8.00
16" diameter bell yoke and crank- $ 10.00
19" diameter bell yoke and wheel- $ 28.00
35" diameter bell yoke and wheel- $120.00
The factory also manufactured Butterfield plough points. The "Economist" reported that they waw some sixty farm, school and church bells ready for hanging in the premises of the Markham Bell Foundry. In the 1870's, a 500-lb bell was shipped to Port Sydney, Nova Scotia, for a church there, and now stands on a cairn in that town's cemetery." There are also index entries for FORSTER's, but not Ann. Anthony, 160, 184; Matthew, 189; Samuel, 208; Wilfrid, 174; William, 160 [Courtesy of Ron Cushman]

1861 Census Whitchurch, York Co
Stephens [sic] Peers [sic[, farmer, b Canada West. F.C. (response to "married during this year?"), Presbyterian, 51
Ann, b England, W. Methodist, 49
William, b Canada West, F. C. Presbyterian, 21
Henrieta, 15
Diana 13
Stephen 6

Stephen died 4 July 1864 in Markham Ontario.

1871 Census Whitchurch, North York Ontario
PEER, Ann b England, W. Meth, widow, English origin
Henrietta, 23 b Ont, German origin (Holland scratched out)
Diannah, 20 b Ont, German origin
Stephen, 15 b Ont, Holland origin

Children of Stephen Peer & Ann Forster

.... 2 **Stephen Thadeus Peer** b: 02 Jan 1856 in Whitchurch, Ontario, d: Aft. 1885
.... +Mary Augusta Abercrombie b: Abt. 1857 in Picton, Ontario, m: 27 Aug 1879 in Hamilton, Ontario, d: Aft. 1885
.... 2 **Barbara Ann Peer** b: 06 Jun 1854
.... 2 **Diannah Augusta (Gussie) Peer** b: 09 Feb 1850 in Ontario
.... 2 **Henrietta J. A. Peer** b: 07 Oct 1845 in Ontario, d: Aft. 1910 in Probably California
.... +Anthony Whitehead b: Sep 1845 in Ontario, m: 1874, d: Aft. 1910
.... 2 **William Peer** b: 19 Jan 1842 in Markham, York Co. Ontario, d: 19 Mar 1917 in Norwood, Asphodel Twp, Peterborough County Ontario
.... +Agnes Nelson b: 08 Aug 1843 in Bloomsfield, Prince Edward County, Ontario, m: 28 May 1868 in Richmond Hill, York Co. Ontario, d: 26 Mar 1930 in Norwood, Asphodel Twp, Peterborough County Ontario
.... 2 **Mary Elizabeth Peer** b: 15 Jun 1839 in Whitchurch, York Co. Ontario, d: Aft. 1900 in Possibly California
.... +William Sangster b: Abt. 1833 in New York City, New York, m: 10 Aug 1855 in York Co. Ontario, d: Aft. 1871
.... 2 **Lydia Rebecca Peer** b: Sep 1838 in Ontario, d: Bet. 1920-1930 in San Francisco, California
.... +Robert Cowan b: 20 Apr 1832 in Scotland, m: 07 Oct 1861 in Stouffville, York Co. Ontario, d: Bet. 1900-1910 in San Francisco, California
.... 2 **John Antone Peer** b: 11 Apr 1836

Edward Peer & Catharine Haggarty

Edward Peer, Pte 2nd Lincoln Militia
Dec 1838 C1040 p 59
Jan 1839 C 1040 p 73

1851 Census Canada West (Ontario)
Province: Canada West (Ontario)
District: Welland County
District Number: 40
Sub-District: Stamford
Sub-District Number: 382
Page: 47
Line: 17
Roll: C_11757
Schedule: A

Welland County, Stamford
Pear, Edward, labourer, b. Stamford, can't read religion, 37
Catherine 32
David 12
John 10
Lydia C. 8
Jane 4
Hannah 1

1861 Census Welland
Pear, Edward, labourer b UC 46
Catharine 41
Stephen 21
William H 2
Jane 13
Hannah 11
Nancy 8
Matilda 5

Obituary: Mrs. Catharine Peer, relict of the late Edward Peer, died at the home of her daughter Mrs. George Learn, Queen Street, age 82 years. For many years she resided at Beechwoods, Stamford Township, and lived in town a short while. One son, John Peer of Park Street and several daughters survive. Steve Peer, the famous rope walker was a son. Funeral to be Dec. 26

William Dalton Records (Sexton of Drummond Hill Cemetery)
26 Dec. 1900. Old Mrs. Peer was buried on the north side of her husband Edward Peer. Her daughter Nancy Peer paid for the funeral

Most of the Learn documents and photogarphs are courtesy of Kathy Morningstar <rkmstar@ @caninet.com>, Learn Family Bible, in possession of Estelle (Stella) Jane Learn 19901-1980s until her death, Mrs. Catherina Peer listed in Death Register of the Learn Bible. She died Dec. 20, 1900.

PEER
Edward Peer, born July 31, 1814, died March 15, 1861, aged 46 years, 7 months and 15 days.

This was a son of Stephen Peer who owned lands in this vicinity early in the last century and after whom Peer Street is named. Stephen Peer served in Capt. John Rowe's company of the 2nd Lincoln and fell with his captain on the disastrous field of Chippawa, July 5th, 1814. His body was left on the field and was probably among those burned by the United States troops. No trace of him was ever found by his family. His widow married one Barker, an early Drummondville merchant, after whom Barker street is named. Edward Peer was born just twenty-six days after his gallant father met his death. A son of Edward Peer was also named Stephen. He won notoriety by walking across the Niagara gorge on a five-eighths inch wire rope. Three days later, June 25th, 1887, he fellfrom the wire to the rocks and was fatally injured.

Source: *Niagara Historical Society*

Children of Edward Peer & Catherine Haggarty

.... 2 Stephen David Peer b: 1840 in Montrose, Stamford Tp. Welland Co. Ontario, d: 25 Jun 1887 in Niagara Falls, Ontario

.... +Catharine Young b: Sep 1844 in Canada, d: Aft. Nov 1910

.... 2 John Peer b: Abt. 1841 in Stamford Tp. Welland Co. Ontario, d: 08 Apr 1902 in Niagara Falls, Welland Co. Ontario

.... +Susan Delila Thomas b: 17 Jan 1845 in Port Robinson, Ontario, m: Bef. 1879, d: 13 May 1916 in Niagara Falls, Welland Co. Ontario

.... 2 Lydia C. Peer b: Bet. 01 Mar 1843-1848 in Stamford, Welland Co. Ontario, d: 24 Sep 1923 in Dunnville, Haldimand Co. Ontario

.... +Mr. McIntosh

.... +Alexander Collins b: Apr 1846 in England, m: Abt. 1877, d: Bet. 1900-01 Nov 1910

.... 2 Louise Jane (Jane) Peer b: 19 Jun 1848 in Stamford, Welland Co. Ontario, d: Aft. 25 Mar 1936

.... +George Henry (Henry) Cadwell b: 08 Sep 1846 in Pekin, New York, m: 31 Jan 1867, d: 25 Mar 1936 in Oakdale, Nebraska

.... 2 Hannah Elizabeth Peer b: 02 Jul 1850 in Stamford Tp. Ontario, d: 09 Dec 1930 in Wainfleet Tp, Welland County Ontario

.... +Lawrence Kadwell b: Abt. 1843 in Ontario, m: Bef. 1874, d: 28 Aug 1903 in Welland County Ontario

.... 2 Nancy Peer b: 26 Oct 1855 in Stamford, Welland Co. Ontario, d: Abt. 1951

.... +John Crawford b: Abt. 1847 in Ireland, m: 27 Sep 1897 in Stamford, Welland Co. Ontario, d: 1901 in Oregon

.... 2 Marian (Maria) Margaret Matilda Peer b: 28 Jan 1856 in Buckwoords, Stamford, Welland Co. Ontario, d: 26 Apr 1930 in Niagara Falls, Ontario

.... +George Learn b: 21 Jun 1855 in Willoughby Tp. Ontario, m: 06 Jan 1880 in Wainfleet Tp. Welland Co. Ontario

.... 2 William Henry Peer b: Jun 1860 in Stamford, Welland Co. Ontario, d: 17 Jun 1940

.... +Armintha Currant b: Apr 1862 in Ontario, m: Abt. 1880, d: Aft. 17 Jun 1940

Documents

of His Majesty's Province of Upper Canada &c. &c. &c

In Council.

The Petition of Lydia Peer of Stamford

Humbly sheweth,

That your Petitioner is the Daughter of Haggai Skinner of Stamford aforesaid an U.E. Loyalist; that she is married to Stephen Peer and has never received any Lands from the Crown.

Therefore your Petitioner prays that your Excellency in Council, may be pleased to grant her two hundred Acres of the Waste Lands of the Crown, and permit the said Stephen Peer of Stamford aforesaid to locate the same and take out the Deed therefor when completed. —

And your Petitioner will ever pray

Lydia peer

Stamford March 1, 1811

Lydia Peer maketh Oath and saith that she is the Daughter of Haggai Skinner of Stamford an U.E. Loyalist; that she is married to Stephen Peer and that she has never received any Lands or Order for Lands from the Crown —

Sworn before me at Stamford   Lydia peer
in the Province of Upper Canada
the 1st Day of March 1811 —

John Reilly J.P.

I do hereby certify that Lydia Peer signed the above Petition in my Presence, that she is the Person she describes herself to be and to the best of my Knowledge and Belief she has never received

1 March 1811 Petition of Lydia Peer of Stamford for land as the daughter of the Loyalist Haggai Skinner. States she is married to Stephen Peer

Civil Secretary's Correspondence, Upper Canada Sundries, May-August 1814. RG5, A1, Vol. 20. 5 July 1814 p 5600.

This document certifies that the husbands of the 10 widows listed were killed in action at Chippewa on 5 July 1814.

Civil Secretary's Correspondence, Upper Canada Sundries, May-August 1814. RG5, A1, Vol. 20. 6 July 1814 p 5602.

This document is a return of the men killed at the Battle of Chippewa plus whether or not they left a widow and children. Stephen Peer's name is on Line 10 with 1 widow and 2 children.

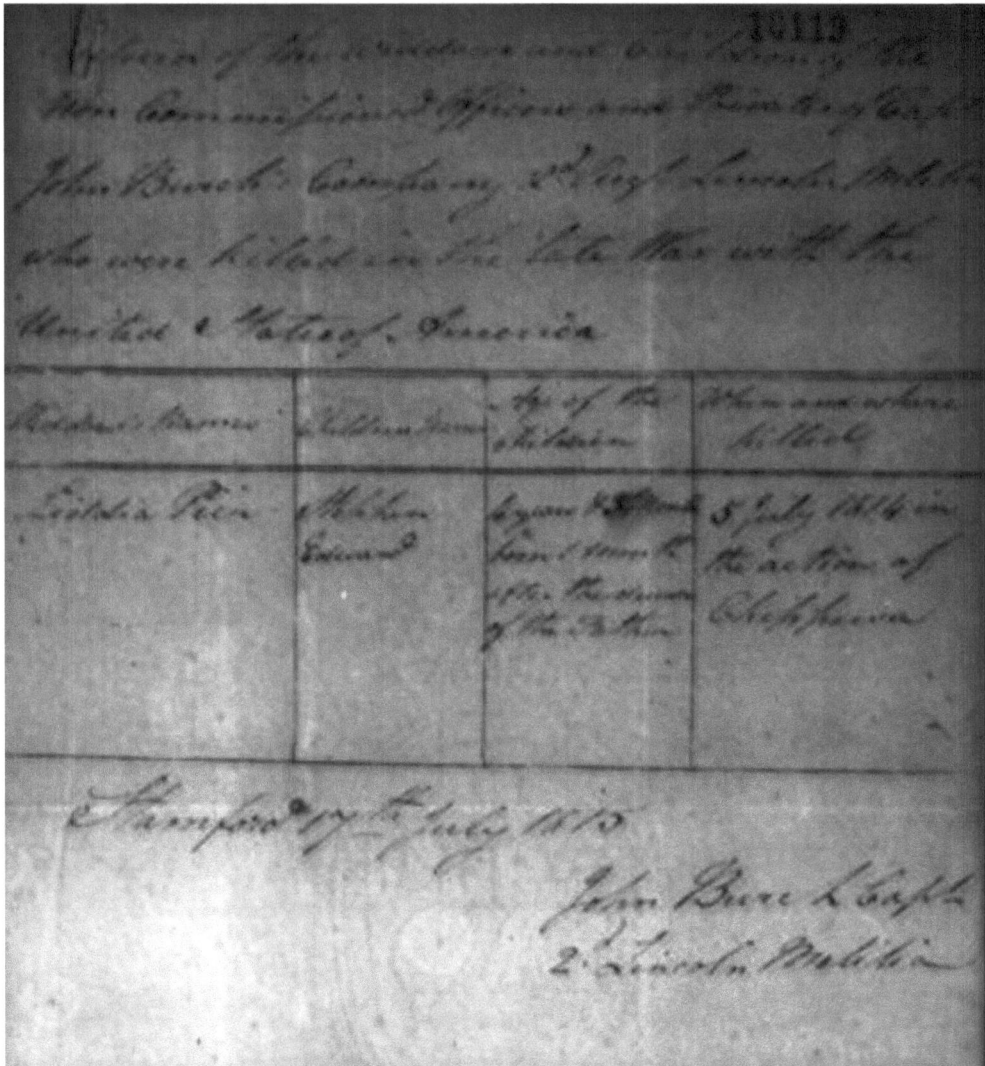

Civil Secretary's Correspondence, Upper Canada Sundries, May-August 1815. RG5, A1, Vol. 23, pp 9798-10423. Stamford, 17 July 1815. p.10119

This document shows that Lydia Peer was the wife of Stephen Peer of the 2nd Lincoln Regiment in the War of 1812. Stephen's death is shown as 5 July 1814 at the Battle of Chippewa. She is now his widow and has two sons - Stephen 4 years old (number of months is obscured) and Edward who was born 1 month after the death of his father.

Widow Adams of David Adams
Widow Taylor of J. Taylor
Widow Bastedo of J. Bastedo
Widow Peer of Stephen Peer
Widow Wilkinson of J. Wilkinson
Widow McDonell of J. McDonell
Widow Forsyth of Sol Forsyth
Widow Turney of Capt. Turney
Widow Blanchett of Louis Blanchett
Widow Skinner since Married

at York has left two or three children
who have got their pension as the
children of the late Sergt. Skinner
who was killed in action the 5 July 1814
and also the husbands of the above
nine widows.

(Signed) Thomas Clark Lt. Col.
Thomas Millin

Certified
Lt. Col. Thomas Millin
Upper Canada

received the above from
Lt. Col. T. Dickson July 17 1816.

Civil Secretary's Correspondence, Upper Canada Sundries July-August 1816, RG5, A1, Vol. 29, pp 13131-13591. Page 13248. July 17, 1816. Widow Peer of Stephen Peer

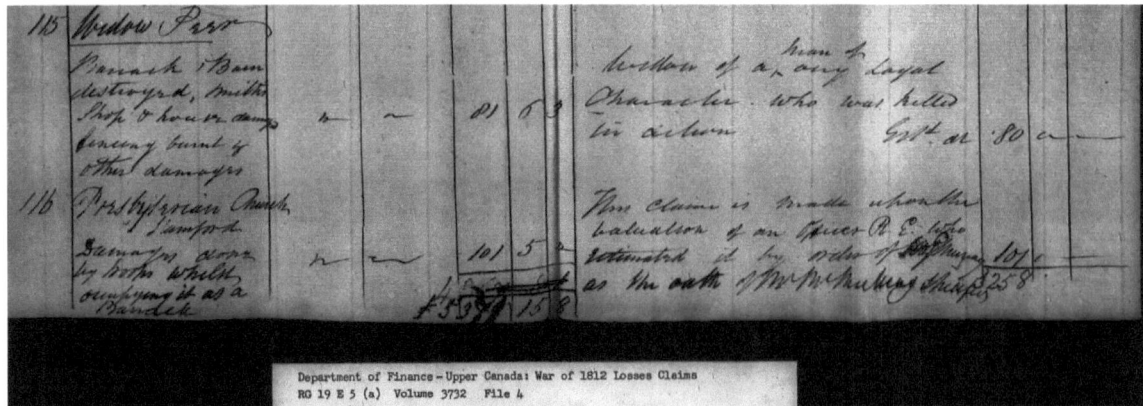

Widow Peer. Barrack and Barn destroyed, -- shop and house damaged, fencing burned & other damages. Notation states "widow of a man of very loyal character who was killed in action" Source: Department of Finance, Upper Canada, War of 1812 Losses Claims, RG19, E5 (a), Vol. 3732, File 4

Widow Peer, of Stamford, Niagara District claims renumeration for wagon, two sets of harnesses, 3 year old horse, 2 saddles and bridle, and wearing apparel taken by enemy in amount 20.097L, 3s, 9p. Awarded 16.448L Source: Department of Finance, Upper Canada, War of 1812 Losses Claims, RG19, E5 (a), Vol. 3733, File 6

17 Jan. 1824 Department of Finance, Upper Canada, War of 1812 Losses Claims, RG19, E5 (a), Vol. 3749,File 3

Aug 2. Co. 252

Widow Ferr –

£91: 17: 6

Estimated at
Eighty pounds –

___

Statement of Property taken from the Widdow
Ferr by the American Troops and Indians in
the american service during the late War with
the United States

1814			£ s d			
July 10th	A Waggon £40 two set of Harness £24		23-0-0	64	"	"
	a Horse aged 5 years		15-0-0	40	"	"
	2 Saddles and 2 Bridles		6-0-0	13	"	"
	5 Wollen Blankets	5-@ 20/	3-	5	"	"
	Wearing apparel		7-10-0	20	"	"
				£	147	

£91.17.6

Class 1. no 115
Widow Peer
Stamford
£ 81: 6: 3

Estimated at
Eighty pounds

Widow Peer Exec[?]
of Class no. 2 No 252

Statement of damages done to the Widow Rie
by the Troops and Indians in his Majesties serv[ice]
between the 1st Septr 1814 and 1st ~~June~~ March 1815

		£ s d	
A Barrack destroyed		5-0-0	20 „ „
A Barn do (damaged)		2-10-0	6 „ ~
damage done Smith Shop & House	3-0-0		12 „ ~
3 Acres of Oates destroy'd by the 97 Regt	5-0-0		12 „ ~
1 Cwt Iron £8-8 Three axes (say two)	£1-12-0 Do 3-0-0	2-12-0	2 „ ~
damage in loss of Seeds & Oates	30 Rails at 2½	1-3-3	
as appraisment		£13-5-3	78 2 „
			N767 £130 2 „

£81.6.3

March 15 - 1815

it apears that Lijda Par of Stamford
has sustaind the loss off one hundread
and thirty one Panels of fence taken
off his primeses and twelve shillins
N Y Curency alowd pr Panel —

Properly asertaind by us —

Saml Van Wyck
and Haggai Cook

131
12
1562
78. 2

Haggia Cook on Oath Saith that he and Samuel Van
Wycke late of Stamford diseased, was called upon
by Mrs Lydia Peir to appraise damages done
to Her Fences — during the late war with the
United States — which damages to the best of his
recollection were done by His Majestys 82nd Regt —
that he signed the within document and that
to the best of his judgment at that time, the
sum of twelve shillings york pr panel, was a
reasonable and fair valuation
sworn before me
this 17th January 1824
Samuel Street J P

Haggai Cook

District
of
Niagara

Personally appeared before me Samuel Street Esquire one of His Majesty's Justices of the Peace — Lydia Barker, late Widow of Stephen Peir deceased — who says On Oath that the losses & damages sustained by her and during the lifetime of her former Husband Stephen Peir deceased, and for which she claims remuneration are just and reasonable — and to the best of her knowledge — the loss & damage was actually sustained for which she claims — remuneration —

Lydia Barker

Sworn before me at Stamford this 17 January 1824

Samuel Street J. P.

Appeared before me Samuel Street Esquire one
of His Majesty's Justices of the Peace for
the District aforesaid – John Misener of Stamford
Wheelwright – who on Oath says that shortly after
the War he was called upon by Mrs Lydia
Peir to view and appraise damages done
to her premises by His Majesty's troops and
during the Action at Lundy's Lane – that
he is known to His Majesty's 82nd Regt being
in occupation of her Barn, Smith's Shop &
House for a considerable length of time during
the latter end of the year 1814 and beginning
of the year 1815 – and farther he says that he
appraised the damages done, in completely
destroying a Barrack, at fifty Dollars –
damages done the Barn at fifteen Dollars
and injury done to her dwelling House
and Smith's Shop at Thirty Dollars –
that he built the waggon for which Mrs
Peir claims remuneration, which he valued
at One hundred Dollars – that to the best
of his judgement and belief, the appraisements
so made by him at that time were just and
reasonable as he then believed –
Sworn before me
this 17th January 1824

Samuel Street J. P.

John Misener

Susan Skinner - Wife of Haggai Skinner of Stamford yeoman, saith On Oath - that during the late War, she thinks in the Summer of 1814 - that her late Father in Law. Haggai Skinner Senior. deceased - went to the premises of his daughter Mrs Lydia Prir - and brought from thence to his own place where deponent they lived sundry Goods, and Articles belonging to Mrs Prir - that they were removed with a view of keeping them from being taken by the enemy - whichwere then in the neighbourhood - that about a week after they were brought to Mr Skinners premises - Three Americans came to the House and took away every thing which was there belonging to Mrs Prir - that among the Articles she recollects - a Waggon - a Horse - a good Set of Harness - a Saddle and Bridle almost new - and sundry other Articles - which she does not now recollect - that she never afterwards saw any of the above her Articles

Sworn before me
at Stamford this 19th
January 1824
Samuel Sent S. P.

Susan + Skinner
mark

Hugh Haggerty of Stamford yeoman on Oath says – that during the late War, Sundry Articles of thins Cloathing belonging to the late Stephen Peir deceased – were deposited with him the deponent for safe keeping – that at the time deponents House was plundered, by the Americans – Indians the whole of the above Articles belonging to Mr Peir were taken off –

Hugh Haggerty
sworn before me 17th January 1824
Samuel Street J. P.

March 19, 1824. Department of Finance, Upper Canada, War of 1812 Losses Claims, RG19, E5 (a), Vol. 3759, File 1. Stephen & Lydia Peer, Stamford, microfilm t-1139, pages 1084-1087 (4 images)

Niagara Falls, March 19, 1824. Dear Sir – the widow of the late Stephen Peer of Stamford who was killed in the Battle of Chippewa – 1814, has requested us to send forward to this Board of Claims her enclosed receipt of Col. – Heron for a horse, saddle and bridle --- or taken from her late husband.

The case is – Pier [sic] who in 1813 and during the war until killed, was very active in harrassing the enemy when in possession of this Niagara Frontier – on 16th June 1813 was -- to this place, he waylaid two American Dragoons mounted on their lame horses, surprised and took them both prisoner, tied them and mounted his horse, and with the assistance of two militia men, marched the two Dragoons up to [Henry's?] at twenty mile Creek, where he delivered them to Lt. Col. De Heron, then commanding there, who took his horse, an excellent one, from Peer, and sent him home on foot. Peer thought himself badly treated in having his horse taken from him, and in his lifetime frequently applied to me to assist in procuring -- --- --- for --- but my leaving the country in Oct. 1813 and his being killed in the summer following, prevented this. The widow, now married to John Barker of Stamford, requests that I should apply to this Board of Claims on her behalf, for any renumeration they may think fit to award her. I have only to add that Peer was receiving – pay – allowances at the time the Dragoons and horses were taken. Your obedient servant, Thomas Clark

Bottom is the receipt from Lt. Col. De Heron for "Received from Stephen Pier a horse, saddle and bridle" dated June 17, 1813

Receipt

Eleanor &c ......

to Stephen Peer

for a Horse saddle &

& Bridle 17th June

1819

1808 (P)
9 February 1808
Bond

Levi Peer
Richard Hatt Esq
Edward Peer
And
Stephen Peer

Estate of John Peer

Conrad Felman
David Kern
Appraisers

Know all men by these presents that we Levi Peer
Richard Hatt Edward Peer and Stephen Peer
all of the County of Lincoln
District of Niagara Province of Upper Canada are held and
firmly bound to the Governor Lieutenant Governor or Person
Administering the Government of the said Province, in the
Sum of One Thousand Pounds of Good and lawful Money
of this Province to be well and truly Paid to the said Governors Lieut Governors or Person Administering the Government
for the time being and for which Payment so to be made
We bind ourselves, Our Heirs, Executors and Administrators
firmly by these Presents Sealed with our Seals and dated
at Niagara this Ninth day of February in the Year of
Our Lord One Thousand Eight Hundred & Eight.

The Condition of this Obligation is such
that if the above bounden Levi Peer Richard Hatt Edward
Peer and Stephen Peer
Administrators of all and the Goods, Chattles
and Credits of John Peer deceased do make
or cause to be made a true and perfect Inventory of all and
Singular the Goods, Chattles, and Credits of the said
John Peer deceased which shall have come
to the hands possession or knowledge of the said Levi Peer
Richard Hatt Edward Peer and Stephen Peer
or into the Hands of any
other Person or Persons, for the said Levi Peer Richard Hatt

Know all men by these present? That we Levi Peer, Richard Hatt, Edward Peer and Stephen Peer all of the County of Lincoln District of Niagara Province of Upper Canada are held and firmly bound to the Governors Lieutenant Governor or Person Administering the Government of the said Province in the Sum of One Thousand £ of Good and Lawful Money, of this Province to be well and truly Paid to the said Governors Lieut. Governors or Person Administering the Government for the time being and for which Payment so to be made we bind ourselves, our heirs, Executors and Administrators firmly by these present Sealed with our Seals and dated at Niagara this Nineth day of February in the Year of our Lord One Thousand Eight Hundred & Eight.

The Condition of this Obligation is such that if the above bound Levi Peer, Richard Hatt, Edward Peer and Stephen Peer, Administrators, of all and the Goods, Chattles and Credits of John Peer, deceased, do make or cause to be made a true and perfect Inventory of all and singular the goods, chattles and credits of the said John Peer, deceased, which shall have come to the hands & possession or knowledge of the said Levi Peer, Richard Hatt, Edward Peer and Stephen Peer, or into the hands of any other Person or Persons for the said Levi Peer, Richard Hatt, Edward Peer and Stephen Peer, or either of them so made do exhibit or cause to be exhibited into the office of the Surrogate of the District of Niagara at or before *the expiration of Six Calendar months from the date of the above written Obligation and the same goods, Chattles and Credits of the asid deceased at the time of his death which at any time after shall come into the hands and possession of the said Levi Peer, Richard Hatt, Edward Peer and Stephen Peer, or into the hands and possession of any other peros or persons for the said Levi Peer, Richard Hatt, Edward Peer and Stephen Peer, then the Obligation to be void and of none effect or else to remain in full force and virtue.*

Signed Levi Peer, Edward Peer, Stephen Peer
Signed and sealed Robert Kerr, --- Smith

We Levi Peer, of Glanford, & Richard Hatt of Ancaster
in the County of Lincoln, & Province of Upper
Canada; Do Swear, that we will Justly, and
truly administer, all and Singular, the Goods
and chattels, rights and credits of John Peer
——— late of Ancaster deceased, and pay all
his Debts, and Legacies as far as his Estate
will Extend, and the Law charge, and
that we will a true inventory make, of
the rights and credits, goods chattels, and Effects
of the said John Peer ——— Deceased, and
Exhibit the same, to such appraisers, as
may be appointed, to appraise and Value
the Same; and that we will with all
convenient speed, the said inventory, together
with the said appraisement, certified under
his Hand

Office of the Surrogate Court, for this District
And we do further, swear, that we do not
know the said John Peer ——— deceased
left any last Will, or testament, in writing
or otherwise, and that we do believe, he
died intestate. So help us God ———
Niagara Surrogate   Levi Peer
Office 9th February
1808

---

*We Levi Peer of Glanford and Richard Hatt of Ancaster, in the County of Lincoln, Province of Upper
Canada, do swear, that we will firmly and truly administer all and singular, the goods and chattels,
rights and credits of John Peer, late of Ancaster, deceased, and pay all his debts and Legacies as far as his
Estate will extend, and the law? Change, and that w will a true inventory make of the rights and credits,
goods and chattels, and effects of the said john Peer, deceased, and exhibit the same, --- Appraisers, as
may be appointed, to apriase and value the same, and that we will with all convenient speed, the said
inventory, together with the said appraisement, certified under [crease in paper obscures this part in
copy but it reads "under the hands of the"] the appraiser – unto the office of the Surrogate Court, for this*

District. And we do further swear that we do not know the said John Peer, deceased, left any Last Will or Testament, in writing or otherwise, and that we do believe he died intestate. So help us God. (signed)
Levi Peer
Niagara Surrogate Office 9th February 1808

	To Robert Kerr, Esquire, Judge of the Surrogate Court for the District of Niagara. The Petition of Livi Pierre [sic] Humbly Sheweth That John Pierre [sic] your Petitioners Brother, died as your Petitioner vierily believes, without a last Will and Testament, Your Petioner being the oldest Brother & next of Kin to the deceased, Humbly prays that Letters of Administration may be granted him to Sell the Estate of said John Pierre [sic], deceased. And your Petioner as in duty bound will ever pray (Signed) Levi Peer Niagara, the 9th day of February 1808

Inventory of the Goods, Chattels and Credits of the late John Peer, taken the 13th of February 1808

Inventory taken by Levi Peer & Richard Hatt, Adminstrators of the Estate of the John Peer deceased & appraised as – warrant to Conrad Fellman & David Keer, 13th Februrary 1808

Inventory taken by Levi Pier & Wall
Hatt Administrator of the Estate of
the John Pier Deceased & appraised as
afteresaid by Conrad Filleman &
David Kerr 13th February 1808 —

1 Horse Colt ab. 3 yrs old	16	
1 Bay Horse 7 "	21	
1 Grey Mare " " "	21	
1 Sett Horse Harness for 2 Horses Compt	4	
1 Cutg. Box Knife &c complete	" 12	
1 Dung Fork & Pitch fork	" 10	
1 Scoop Shovel 1 Empty barrel	" 12	
1 Bee	" 1	
1 piece of a Chain	" 11	
1 Sow & three pigs	2 17	
1 Wood Sleigh	1 "	
1 Cow	2 8	
1 Plough & Irons with Irons	2 4	
1 Harrow with 9 Iron teeth	1 "	
3 Hogs in aften fattning	" 8	
1 Grinding Stone	1 "	
1 Grindstone	1 8	

1 Barrel about half full of Beef	1	
2 Barrels with flour & 1 Dr. ab ½ W. Salt	2 13	
1 Barr. 1 vegetable & Bake tray	" 8	
2 Wash Benches & some Soap Fat	1 4	
Walnut Scantling for 4 Bed Steads	" 12	
1 Little Wheel	1 4	
Some Wool & a peg	" 4	
1 Turning Lath	" 10	
9 Walnut boards	" 6	
2 Barrels & some Crout	" 4	
Some Potatoes about 2 Bushl	" 6	
3 Bushl. Potatoes buried	" 9	
1 Box of Paint	" 2	
1 Rifle Powder Horn & Shot bag	6	
Some dryed Beef	" 8	
1 pr. Hand Irons, Shovel & tongs	2	
1 Tea Kettle	1	
8 Old Chairs	1 4	
1 Spade	" 8	
1 Iron Pot	" 15	
2 Trammels	" 4	
1 Wash Tub	" 6	
1 Iron bound Keg	" 2	
1 Frying pan 4/. Knot bowl 2/	" 6	

Brot. over		
2 Flat Irons	8	
1 Knot Reel	" 4	
1 pr. Wool Cards	" 2	
1 Flax seed Seive	" 3	
1 pr. Small Stilyards	" 8	
1 Churn Stand Pork in it	" 14	
1 Gum with dryed Apples	" 6	
1 Bible 3 Books & some by some	" 6	
1 Basket	" 1	
1 Keg about half full Whitelead	" 10	
1 Crock & Some Honey	" 4	
1 Sett Smith & King Screws	" 6	
1 Nail Box with Sundries in it	" 6	
2 pr. Cakes of Tallow	" 10	
1 Walnut Table & Candles in drawer	1 4	
1 Bucket 1 2/ 1 Mauld & rings 5/	" 7	
1 Pump augr. & Taper bit	2 10	
1 Bake oven Shovel 12/- Iron pot 14/	1 6	
1 Saddle & Bridle	1 10	
1 Keyler & Broad Hoe	0 7	
1 Small walnut Chest	" 16	
5 Hives & 1 Crane	2 2	
1 Adze Broad axe & Hand axe	1 8	
4 Augers 2 In. 1 - ¾ - & ½ In	1 6	
4 Planes	1 1	
1 Plough & Groove	" 18	
1 Axe & 1 Chest & Tools	6	
1 Skimmer & Beef fork	" 6	
1 Copping axe & Iron & Chill	" 10	

Brought forward		
Wheat on the Ground 8 W. Sowing		
Rye Do. Do. 4 " "		
Rye in the Barn		
Rye on Shares at & Skinners		
John Smiths note —	2. 11.	
Balance on P Gordons Do. —	5.	
Lewis's Note —	2. 10. 4	
Henry Millers note —	" 7	—
Wm. Kilmores Do. —	5	—
Balce. on Barth. Swets note	" 9	
Jsl. Moodys note	" 12. 9	
Andw. Templetons Do. —	5. 15. 6	
Miller Lawrasen Note —	" 3	
Henry Young —	1	
Mr. McMullins halt	" 5. 9	
D. in the various notes —	9. 18. —	
Edm Smith		
Jacob Smoak		
Jonathan Onsted —	" 10	
W. Forge	" 4	
	209. 7. 5 —	

1 horse colt abt 3 years old

1 Bay horse

1 Gray Mare

1 set Horse Harness for 2 horses complete

1 Cu—Box Knife – complete

1 Dung? Fork & Pitchfork

1 Scoop Shovel & Empty barrel

1 box

1 piece of a chain

1 S—H-- --

1 Wood Sleigh

1 C—

1 Plough & Irons with _ivis

1 Harrow with 9 –

3 Hogs in a pen fatting

1 Hive of Bees

1 Grinder –

1 Soap Tub Bucket & K—ler

1 barrel about half full of Beef

2 Barrel with flour & 1 do? [ditto?] – Salt

1 Barrel 1 Deye? Tub & 1 B—of Hay

2 Work Benches & Some Soap, --

Walnut Scandling? for 4 Bedsteads

1 Little Wheel

Some Wool & a Keg

1 Turning Lathe

9 Walnut boards

2 Barrels & some Crout?

Some potatoes about 2 bushels

2 Bushels Potatoes, burried

1 Box of paint

1 Rifle, Powder Horn & Shot Bag

Some Dryed Beef

1 pr Hand Irons, Shovel & Tongs

1 Tea Kettle

8 old Chains

1 Spade

1 Iron Pot

2 Trammels?

1 Wash Tub

1 Iron Bound Keg

1 Frying Pan 4/. Knot bowl 2/

2 Flat Irons

1 Knot E—

1 pr wool cards

2 pr cakes of Tallow

1 Walnut Table with Candles in drawer

1 Bucket 2/ 1 Maul & Rings? 5/

1 Pump Auger & Ta—Bit

1 bake Oven & Bail? 12/ Iron Pot 24/

1 Saddle & Bridle

1 Keglor & Bra—Hoe

1 Small walnut chest

5 Hives & 1 Ba—

1 Adze, Broad Axe & Hand Axe

4 Augers

4 Planes

1 Plough & Gr—

1 Axe & 1 Chest of Tools

1 Skimmer & Beef Fork

1 Copping Axe & Conk Shell

1 – Trowel & Graining Knife

Cauldron

BedStead -- & Bed –

1 ox bell & hand saw?

Crockery Wine Glasses

Tumblers & Decanturs

1 earthen Jug

2 Pewter Basins & Pewter Plates & Knives & forks

Spoons -- & E-- & Be—complete

1 coat & 2 flannel shirts

2 pr Coveralls & Shirt Jacket

4 Waistcoats & 2 muslin Shirts

2 pr socks

1 hat

1 auger

1 small Stack—Wheat

Wheat in the barn

Part of a stack of Hay

Wheat Ground & Wheat Sowing

Rye (ditto)

Rye in the barn

Bus—Shares & I. Skinners

John Smiths note

Balance on P. Jordon's ditto [note]

Serviss's –

Henry Millers Note

Wm Killman's note

Balance on Bar—Sweet's note

1 Flax Seed Veine	*J—Leodys? –*
1 pr small Halyards	*Andrew Tunf—ditto*
1 Churn, some pork in it	*Miller? Laurason –*
1 Green? with dryed Apples	*Henry Young*
1 Bible, 3 Books & Employ—	*M. McMullins –*
1 Basket	*David Newtons –*
1 Keg about half full white lead	*E—m Smith*
1 Crock & some Honey	*Jacob Smoak*
1 SexthSmith & Ring? & Wedges	*Jonathan Omstead*
1 Nail Box with Sundries in it	*W. Tonger*

Photographs & Newspaper Clippings

Laura Peer

Lawrence Ellman Learn & Bella Smith

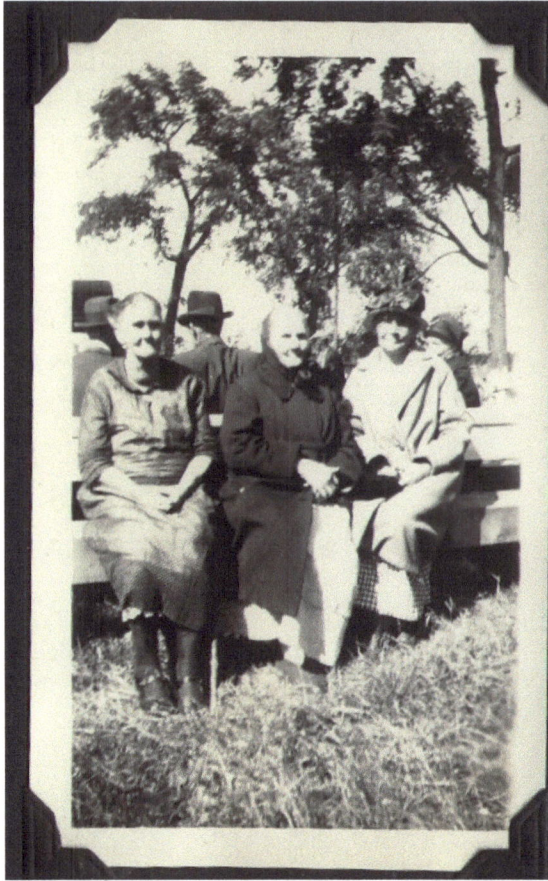
Maria Matilda Learn nee Peer & two sisters

N. Learn

Unknown, Rosanna, Mildred, Maria, Estella Learn

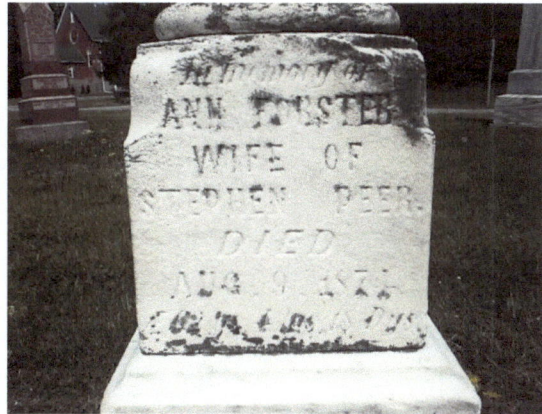

Stephen Peer & Ann Forster Tombstones in Locust Hill Cemetery, Markham Ontario

Living Memorials

THE finest in art, music, literature, architecture and sculpture portrays the heart throbs of a thousand generations as they sought to memorialize their heroes and loved ones. The Pyramids, Taj Mahal, Rheims, Saint Peter's, Westminster Abbey and Vimy Memorial in the Old World are a few of the living tributes to those who have passed on. In Canada and the United States (in the New World), the Washington and Lincoln Memorials, the monument to Champlain at Orillia, Ontario, that to General Brock at Queenston, Ontario; the Peace Tower at Ottawa; Hart House Memorial Tower at the University of Toronto; all enrich life and remind us that we are the heirs of a great past.

Not only do we believe in God, and a future life of peace, happiness and beauty surpassing human conception; but we also feel that in remembering these worthy ones we are able to attain new heights and to challenge posterity to even greater accomplishments.

Let us remember, therefore, that while we gather to pay our parting tribute and to bring solace and comfort to the sorrowing, we have also come to consecrate ourselves anew to the great unfinished task of creating a better world.

Here in the sanctity of love and memory let us seek to sustain the relatives and close friends by the evidencing of faith and hope; to draw a little closer in friendship and understanding; to inspire the bereaved with greater courage for the days ahead; and to paint a memory picture that shall ever remain a source of comfort and strength.

Memorial Services

For
MRS. GEORGE WESLEY LEARN
(Florence Elizabeth Current)

Born
Niagara Falls, New York
February 14, 1902

Passed Away
Niagara Falls, New York
Wednesday, December 25, 1974

Services held at
Hetherington & Deans Funeral Chapel
Saturday, December 28, 1974, at 3 p.m.

Officiant
Rev. Robert Mailey

Music by
Mr. Harold Revill

Interment
Fairview Cemetery

Directors
A. J. DEANS — W. J. FEAVER

BIRTHS

George Learn   June 21st   1855.

Maria Matilda Learn " Jan. 28th   1856

Nancy Cathrine Learn " March 28th   1881

Henry Jacob Learn   March 16th   1883.

William Edward Learn   Nov 23th   1885.

Lawrence Ellman Learn   Jan 13th   1889.

Jean May Learn   May 14th   1891.

George Westly Learn   Sept 26th   1894.

Charles Lewes Learn   March 3th   1898

Estella Jane Learn   Dec 9th   1901

Mildred Florence Mable Donald Feb 10th 1909.

John Frederick William Donald Mar 31. 1912

Gorden William Donald Nov 3 1914.

Phylis Elanor Morningstar — Aug. 12, 1928

Clayton Donald Morningstar May 13-1930

Douglas Morningstar Dec 18-1931

Howard   "   Jan 19-1934

Cathrine   "   Feb 8   1936

Robert   "   Oct 28   1937

MARRIAGES

George Learn and Maria Matilda Peer Married
January 6th 1880.

Henry Jacob Learn and LuElla Barr.
Married June 25th 1908.

Maye Irene Learn and John Robert Donald
Married December 29th 1908.

Nancy Learn and J.W. Fero
married Oct 20th 19.10.

Lawrence Ellman Learn and Bella smith
Married Dec 29th 1927

Mildred Florence Mable Donald and Clayton Morningstar
Married May 24th 1928.

George Wesley Learn and Florence E. Lewis
Married

DEATHS

Lillian Learn Died Feb 27th 1888.

Mrs Catherine Peer Died Dec 20th 1900

Charls L. C Learn Died July 22nd 1908

William. J. Learn Died August 23th 1908

Maria Matilda Learn. Died April 26, 1930.

George Learn Died June 1st 1931

Faunce Ellman Died June 2nd 1954

George Westly Died Feb 23 1962

Henry Jacob March 1st 1963

May S Donald Nov 4 th 1969

Nancy Catherine Fero August 2, 1974

Florence Elizabeth Learn December 25, 1974

William Jess Fero Dec 27th 1957

Marriage Certificate.

I hereby Certify that _George Learn_ of the Township of _Willoughby_ County of _Welland_ and _Maria Matilda Beer_ of the Township of _Stamford_ County of _Welland_ were married by me, a Minister of the United Brethren Church, at the residence of _Lawrence Cadwell_ of the Township of _Wainfleet_ County of _Welland_ on the _sixth_ day of _January 1880_ in presence of

Edward J. Green
Nancy A. Beer } WITNESSES

Jacob McComb

Minister of the United Brethren Church.

"Monck Reform Press," Dunnville, Ont.

43

Eighty Years Or More
Mrs. Nancy Fero

Friends and neighbors gathered at the Buckley Avenue home of Mrs. Nancy Fero on Tuesday afternoon and evening to honor her on the occasion of her 80th birthday.

The octogenarian was born March 28, 1881 in Netherby. Her parents were G e o r g e and Matilda Learn, and she had five brothers and three sisters. Two brothers and two sisters are still living. They are, Jacob, this city; Wesley, Niagara Falls, N.Y.; Mrs. May Donald and Miss Estelle Learn, this city.

When Mrs. Fero was about even or eight, the family moved this city, and she was raised the family home on St. Lawnce Avenue. She was a student Simcoe Street School.

In 1909 Nancy Learn was married to William J. Fero in Jepn Street Baptist Church. They oved to her present home on uckley Avenue, where she will ve lived 40 years this August. r. Fero who worked with the .N.R., passed away December 7, 1951.

Mrs. Fero, who is in good health, except for a weak heart which limits her activities, enjoys sewing and crocheting, fancy needlework. She also does all her own housework. She is a member of Esther Rebekah Lodge, The Mothers' Circle of St. Andrew's United Church and the Golden Hour Club.

MRS. NANCY FERO

75 Years In This City

H. JACOB LEARN

Henry Jacob Learn, 81, a resident of this city for the past 75 years, died Monday at his home at 829 Ontario Avenue.

Born in Netherby, Willoughby Township, he had been a carpenter all of his life, working with various contractors and was the oldest active member of the Carpenter's Union.

Mr. Learn was a member of Christ Church, St. Mark's Lodge 105, A.F. and A.M., Mount Nebo Chapter, and the Cataract Lodge No. 103, I.O.O.F.

Predeceased by his wife the former Luella Barr Dec. 1958, he is survived by a son Edward of this city, five grandchildren, Charles E., Jr., Gloria Beverly, Marjorie, and Faith all of Niagara Falls, N.Y., and Daniel of this city, and three sisters, Mrs. Nancy Fero, Mrs. Mae Donald and Miss Estelle Learn all of this city.

Funeral service will be held at the Hetherington and Deans Funeral Chapel Thursday at 1:30 p.m. Tonight at 7:30 St. Mark's Lodge will hold a memorial service in the Chapel and the Cataract Lodge will hold another service Wednesday evening at the same time and place. Interment will be made in Fairview Cemetery.

LEARN — At the Greater Niagara General Hospital, Niagara Falls, Ont. on Monday, Dec. 22, 1958, Luella Barr Learn beloved wife of Henry Jacob Learn and dear mother of Charles E. Learn, Niagara Falls, Ont., aunt of Mrs. Florence Reid, Windsor, Ont. also surviving are 5 grandchildren.

Mrs. Learn is resting at the funeral chapel of Hetherington & Deans, Victoria Ave. Service in the chapel on Sat., Dec. 27th at 2 p.m. Interment in Fairview Cemetery. On Friday evening at 7 o'clock Bluebell Rebekah Lodge will hold a memorial service in the chapel and at 7.30 p.m. Queen of Sheba Chapter O.E.S. will hold a memorial service in the chapel.

23-26

Wedding Bells

LEARN.

A very pretty home wedding took place at Niagara Falls Wednesday evening at the residence of Mr. and Mrs. George Learn of No. 9 St. Lawrence-avenue, when their eldest daughter, Nancy Catherine, was married to Mr. William Jesse Fero, also of this city. The ceremony was performed by the Rev. A. P. Kennedy at 8 o'clock in the presence of 50 friends and relatives of the bridal couple. The bride was gowned in a travelling suit of gray. Her maid of honor, Miss Edith Fero, wore cream crepe de chine. Mr. Elmer Learn acted as best man. Miss Lena Shapland of this city, played the wedding march. At the conclusion of the ceremony supper was served, the table being decorated with smilax and ferns. Mr. and Mrs. Fero left on the 12.01 train for Detroit and Grand Rapids, amid a shower of rice and confetti.

Ozias Learn Laid at Rest.

The funeral of Ozias Learn took place yesterday at one o'clock from the home of his brother, Mr. George Learn, of 9 St. Lawrence avenue. The burial was at Doan's Ridge Cemetery. The bearers were Jacob Learn, W. Learn, E. Learn, W. Ferris, and C. E. Morningstar.

45

IN MEMORIAM

LEARN — In loving memory of our dear mother, Mrs. G. W. Learn who passed away one year ago today, April 26th, 1930.

A wonderful mother, woman and aid,
One who was better God never made,
A wonderful worker so loyal and true,
One in a million—that Mother was you.

Just in your judgment, always right,
Honest and liberal, ever upright
Loved by your friends and all whom you knew,
Our wonderful Mother, that Mother was you.

—Sadly missed by Husband, Daughters and Sons.   25

DIED

AIKENS — At Niagara Falls, Ont., on Monday, March 8th, 1937, Catherine Matilda, beloved wife of Thomas H. Aikens, aged sixty-eight years, mother of Mrs. Grant Haymes, Miss Nellie Aikens, of this city; Mrs. E. Poole, and Mrs. A. L. Chrisman of Niagara Falls, N.Y., and Milbert Aikens of Welland, Ont.; sister of Mrs. Henry Laubocker of Niagara Falls, N.Y., Mrs. Andrew Shauntz, William Kadwell, Lawrence Kadwell, and Charles Kadwell of Wainfleet, and Freeman Kadwell of Port Colborne, Frank Kadwell, Buffalo, N.Y. The funeral will take place from the family residence, 2065 Ross Street on Thursday afternoon at two o'clock and proceed to All Saint's Church for service at two-fifteen. Rev. Percival Mayes will officiate. Interment will be made in the Church cemetery.   9-10

MRS. FORCE DIES

Member of Pioneer Canadian Family Succumbs to Lingering Illness

Mrs. Hanna May Force, 53 years old, wife of Glenn Clayton Force, died at her home, 1115 Pierce avenue, early today following a lingering illness.

Mrs. Force was a member of one of the pioneer families of the Niagara peninsula and was the youngest daughter of the late John and Susan Peer. She was born in Niagara Falls, Ont., and came to this city following her marriage 31 years ago. She had gained a wide circle of friends during her residence in this city and was a member of the Order of the Ladies of the Maccabees.

She is survived by one son, Carl Clayton Force, one daughter, Mrs. Hugh Waters, and one grandson, all of this city, and two sisters, Mrs. Velma Lizmore, Niagara Falls, Ont., and Mrs. Nancy Newman, Stamford, Ont.

Funeral services will be held from the family home Sunday at 2 p. m., with the Rev. Gustav Deimer officiating. Interment will be in Memorial Park cemetery.

Euchre party tonict

OBITUARY

MRS. MARIA MATILDA LEARN

An old and esteemed resident of this city passed away today in the person of Mrs. Maria Matilda Learn, aged seventy-four years. Mrs. Learn had lived in this city for the past thirty-nine years. She was born in Buckwoods. She was a member of the Daughters of St. George. Surviving are her husband George Learn, three sons and five daughters, Mrs. William Fero, Mrs. John Donald, Miss Estella Learn, Jacob, Elmer and Wesley, all of this city ....three sisters, Mrs. Henry Kadwell, Oakdale, Nebraska, Mrs. Hanna Kadwell, Winger, Ont., Mrs. Nancy Crawford, of this city; one brother, William Peer of Niagara Falls, N.Y., and four grandchildren, Mrs. C. Morningstar, John F. Donald, Gordon W. Donald, Edward Learn; one great granddaughter, Phyllis Morningstar. The funeral will take place from the family home 611 St. Lawrence Avenue, on Tuesday, April 29 at two p.m. Interment will be made at Fairview Cemetery.

MRS. LEARN FUNERAL

Obsequies Conducted Under Auspices of Daughters of St. George.

NIAGARA FALLS, Ont., April 30— Very largely attended was the funeral service held yesterday afternoon at 2 o'clock of Maria M. Learn wife of George Learn at the family home 611 St. Lawrence avenue. Rev. Norman McMurray officiated. Interment was in Fairview cemetery. The bearers were Andrew Shauntz, William Kadwell, Freeman Kadwell, Kelly Morningstar, George Fero, Charles Peer.

The service at the home and grave was in charge of the Daughters of St. George, Rose of Niagara Chapter 205 with the following officiating—President, Mrs. Gilbert Jackson, Chaplain Mrs. Robert Barr. There was a profusion of beautiful floral tributes from friends, relatives and organizations. Mrs. Learn being an highly esteemed resident of this city for many years.

Lawrence E. Learn

Lawrence E. Learn, of 536 Welland Avenue, veteran of World War One and retired city employee, died yesterday at the Greater Niagara General Hospital following a long illness. He was 67.

Born in Willoughby Township, Mr. Learn had made his home in Niagara Falls since he was two years old. For 30 years, he was a machinist at the Glendening Lumber Mill. He retired as an employee of the city in August, 1954. Mr. Learn served with the Canadian Army in the First World War and was a member of the Canadian Legion Branch 51. He was an adherent of Jepson Street Baptist Church.

Surviving are three sisters, Mrs. William Fero (Nancy), Mrs. John Donald (Mae), and Miss Estelle Learn, all of this city, and two brothers, Jacob of this city, and Wesley, Niagara Falls, N.Y.

Mr. Learn is resting at the Morse and Son chapel where funeral services will be held tomorrow at two p.m. Interment will be in Fairview cemetery.

Estelle

Many happy returns of your birthday

with love

aunt Nan Cranford

Dec. 1933

DONALD — At Greater Niagara General Hospital on Tuesday, November 4, 1969, Mae I. Donald of 533 Welland Ave., Niagara Falls, beloved wife of the late John Robert Donald, dear mother of Gordon W. Donald, St. Catharines, Ontario, Mrs. Clayton Morningstar (Mildred) Niagara Falls and the late John F. Donald. Sister of Mrs. William Fero (Nancy) and Miss Estelle Learn, both of Niagara Falls. Also surviving are 11 grandchildren and 16 great grandchildren.

Resting at the Morse and Son Chapel where the funeral service will be held on Friday, November 7, at 2 p.m. Interment in Fairview Cemetery. Friends will be received at the Funeral Home 2-4 p.m. and 7-9 p.m.

6

Lawrence E. Learn

Lawrence E. Learn, of 536 Welland Avenue, veteran of World War One and retired city employee, died yesterday at the Greater Niagara General Hospital following a long illness. He was 67.

Born in Willoughby Township, Mr. Learn had made his home in Niagara Falls since he was two years old. For 30 years, he was a machinist at the Glendening Lumber Mill. He retired as an employee of the city in August, 1954. Mr. Learn served with the Canadian Army in the First World War and was a member of the Canadian Legion Branch 51. He was an adherent of Jepson Street Baptist Church.

Surviving are three sisters, Mrs. William Fero (Nancy), Mrs. John Donald (Mae), and Miss Estelle Learn, all of this city, and two brothers, Jacob of this city, and Wesley, Niagara Falls, N.Y.

Mr. Learn is resting at the Morse and Son chapel where funeral services will be held tomorrow at two p.m. Interment will be in Fairview cemetery.

LEARN — At the Greater Niagara General Hospital on Sunday, June 3, 1956, Lawrence Ellman Learn, in his 68th year, of 536 Welland Ave., dear brother of Mrs. William Fero (Nancy), Mrs. John Donald (Mae), Estelle Learn and Jacob Learn, all of this city and Wesley Learn of Niagara Falls, N.Y.

Resting at the Morse & Son Chapel where funeral service will be held on Tuesday, June 5th at 2 p.m. Interment Fairview Cemetery.

MRS. JOHN DONALD
Active lodge member

Mrs. John Robert Donald (Mae), 533 Welland Ave., who was active in fraternal circles, died Tuesday at the Greater Niagara General Hospital.

Born in Niagara Falls, she lived here all her life.

She was a member of St. Andrew's United Church.

She belonged to the Laura Secord Lodge, LOBA 161; the Blue Bell Rebekah Lodge 68; the Niagara Chapter 676 of the Women of the Moose.

She was also a member of the Rapids cribbage team and the Golden Hour Club.

Her husband, John Robert Donald, died in 1936.

One son John F. also predeceased her.

Surviving are one son, Gordon W., St. Catharines; one daughter, Mrs. Clayton Morningstar (Mildred), Niagara Falls; two sisters, Mrs. William Fero (Nancy) and Miss Estelle Learn, both of Niagara Falls; 11 grandchildren and 16 great grandchildren.

Mrs. Donald is at the Morse and Son Chapel where funeral service will be held Friday at 2 p.m.

Burial will be in Fairview cemetery.

TO THE GRAVE

MRS. MARIA M. LEARN

Very largely attended funeral services for the late Mrs. Maria M. Learn were held yesterday afternoon at the family home 611 St. Lawrence Avenue. Rev. Norman McMurray officiated The funeral was in charge of the Daughters of St. George, Rose of Niagara Chapter 205, Mrs. Gilbert Jackson, president; Mrs. Robert Barr, Chaplain. Interment was made at Fairview Cemetery. The pall bearers were: Andy Shauntz, William Kadwell, Freeman Kadwell, Kelly Morningstar, George Fero, Charles Peer.

DIED

LEARN—At Niagara Falls, Ontario, on Saturday, April 26th, 1930, Maria Matilda, beloved wife of George Learn, age 74 years.

The funeral will take place from the family home, 611 St. Lawrence Ave., on Tuesday, April 29th, at 2 p.m. Interment at Fairview cemetery.

Old Resident Buried

NIAGARA FALLS, Ont., June 5.— Funeral service for George Learn, a life long resident of this city, was held at 2 o'clock yesterday afternoon at his late home 611 St. Lawrence avenue which was attended by a great many friends. Rev. Norman McMurray, pastor of Kitchener street United church officiated and burial was in Fairview cemetery. The casket was banked with a great many flowers. The bearers were William Shapland, Joseph Jepson, Isaac McNiven, William Donaki and David Richardson.

Eighty Years Or More
Henry Learn

Henry Jacob Learn, who recently celebrated his 80th birthday, likes nothing better than to sit out on the front steps of his home at 829 Ontario Ave. and enjoy the sunshine.

When the sun is not shining, Mr. Learn takes a stroll down Queen St., as far as his rheumatism will permit, just to see if any of his friends are around.

Mr. Learn was born in Willoughby Township and attended school there for a short time before his family moved to this city.

After attending Simcoe St. Public School, Mr. Learn became an apprentice carpenter and machine hand with a Mr. Carnochan at the corner of St. Lawrence Ave. and Queen St. He stayed there for 20 years and then travelled around Canada.

When he returned to this city he married the former Luella Barr. He worked for a number of companies in the area, retiring 10 years ago.

Mr. Learn has been a member of the Carpenters' Union for 61 years, an Oddfellow for 57 years and a mason for 4 years. He is also a member of Christ Church.

Mrs. Learn died in December 1958.

HENRY LEARN

DONALD — Funeral services for the late Mrs. Mae Donald were held from the Morse and Son Chapel on Friday, November 7th at 2 p.m., with Rev. John Griffen, minister of St. Andrews United Church officiating, assisted by Rev. Dr. William Fingland, Miss Maude Crysler presided at the organ. Interment took place in Fairview Cemetery. The pallbearers, all grandsons of Mrs. Donald were Douglas Morningstar, Howard Morningstar, George Morningstar, Gordon Morningstar, Kenneth Morningstar and Gary Donald.

MRS. LEARN FUNERAL

Obsequies Conducted Under Auspices of Daughters of St. George.

NIAGARA FALLS, Ont., April 30—Very largely attended was the funeral service held yesterday afternoon at 2 o'clock of Maria M. Learn wife of George Learn at the family home 611 St. Lawrence avenue. Rev. Norman McMurray officiated. Interment was in Fairview cemetery. The bearers were Andrew Shauntz, William Kadwell, Freeman Kadwell, Kelly Morningstar, George Fero, Charles Peer.

The service at the home and grave was in charge of the Daughters of St. George, Rose of Niagara Chapter 205 with the following officiating—President, Mrs. Gilbert Jackson. Chaplain Mrs. Robert Barr. There was a profusion of beautiful floral tributes from friends, relatives and organizations. Mrs. Learn being an highly esteemed resident of this city for many years.

OBITUARY

GEORGE LEARN

An old resident of Niagara Falls passed away in the person of George Learn, seventy-six years old, who has lived in the city for the past forty-two years. Mr. Learn was born in Willoughby and lived there for some years until he came here. He had been an invalid for the past sixteen years. Surviving are three sons and three daughters, Mrs. William Fero, Mrs. John Donald, both of this city, Miss Estella, at home, Jacob this city, Elmer and Wesley, at home.

The funeral will be held from the family home 617 St. Lawrence Avenue on June 4 at two p.m. The interment will be made at Fairview Cemetery.

OBITUARY

GEORGE LEARN

An old resident of Niagara Falls passed away in the person of George Learn, seventy-six years old, who has lived in the city for the past forty-two years. Mr. Learn was born in Willoughby and lived there for some years until he came here. He had been an invalid for the past sixteen years. Surviving are three sons and three daughters, Mrs. William Fero, Mrs. John Donald, both of this city, Miss Estella, at home, Jacob this city, Elmer and Wesley, at home.

The funeral will be held from the family home 617 St. Lawrence Avenue on June 4 at two p.m. The interment will be made at Fairview Cemetery.

Handwritten note:
Dec 26" Old Mrs Peer was buried on
The North Side of her Husband
Edward Peer a nice funeral and
[?] Nancy Peer her daughter left
money to bring her [Crawford?] [?]
minister Rev

[left margin handwriting] undertaker M. Morse [?] $3.50 paid

Mrs. Catharine Peer, relict of the late Edward Peer, died at the home of her daughter, Mrs. Geo. Learn, Queen street, on Thursday, at the advanced age of 82 years. Deceased was a resident of "Beechwoods," Stamford township, for many years, and had only resided in town for a short time. She had been ailing for a long time, and on Wednesday suffered a severe paralytic stroke, which caused her death on Thursday. One son, John Peer, Park street, and several daughters survive. Steve Peer, the famous rope walker, who was killed in the gorge some years ago, was a son. The funeral will be held on Wednesday, December 26th, to Lundy's Lane cemetery.

Eighty years or more
Mrs. Nancy Newman

The lack of water flowing over the American Falls does not impress Mrs. Nancy Newman, 90, of 1993 Thorold Stone Rd.

She has seen the cataract stilled before.

It froze over one winter many years ago.

This incident is an example of the many events Mrs. Newman remembers in what the younger generation might call Niagara Fall's "ancient history".

Born in Winger, in 1897, she came to this city at age two. Her father established a shoemaking business and operated a store on Erie Avenue for a few years before becoming a contractor and painter.

Sunday was Mrs. Newman's 90th birthday, and her sons took her to the Skylon Tower for a family dinner.

Monday some old friends of the Day Spring Auxiliary of the United Church threw a party for her; birthday cake and all.

The latest addition to her home is a small but ferocious french poodle named Cassius — you guessed it, after the boxer. "He's a loyal watchdog," she says, and after five seconds in her house, one believes her.

Whatever his bite, the bark is worse.

Back in the days when the Evening Review was still a weekly paper, she worked for the Record before it was taken over by the Review.

"I was an office jockey," she says, doing reporting and keeping the accounts.

"Everybody in the city knew everybody else in those days, not like now," she adds, with a touch of regret.

Those were the days when Thorold Stone was a cinder path, and local residents used septic tanks.

One of the favorite pastimes was to ride on the street car along the gorge, or to take one of the boats to Toronto to see the exhibition.

"There have been great changes . . . great changes."

Mrs. Newman has three sons, Moris and Dr. Charles, both of Dorchester Rd., and William at home. Another son Jackie died at an early age.

She also has two granddaughters and a grandson.

Mrs. Newman is a descendant of the Pennsylvania Dutch and a pioneer family. She is the last member of her family still living; her husband died in 1960.

Many years ago, she used her home as a tourist residence; in the era when $1 could get you a clean bed for the night, and 50 cents a good bacon-and-egg breakfast, "with all the coffee they could drink."

The former Nancy Peer, Mrs. Newman has an impressive list of local ancestors.

Her great-grandfather fought with Butler's Rangers and was killed in the battle of Chippawa.

Peer Street was named after her grandfather, and Barker St. took its name from his widow, Mary Peer Barker.

Because of a hip injuy 16 years ago, Mrs. Newman has been forced to slow down a little. She no longer rents rooms to tourists, but believes in keeping active.

"Activity is what's kept me living and I don't want to become a vegetable with people waiting on me," she says.

For 20 years she wore glasses, until she started doing eye exercises.

Today, at age 90, she still does not need glasses, and her hearing is perfect.

[bear article fragment]
...ecies of bear are the Syrian ...has a ring of white fur ...d the spectacled bear of ...h gets its name from the ...round its eyes.
...dered a delicacy by some ...s a strong flavor and is ...s are used for rugs and ...nd hats.

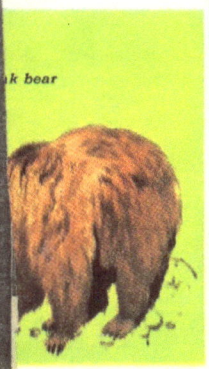

...k bear

[buoyancy article fragment]
...dition of positive buoyancy. A ...it weighs more than the weig... ...displaces. A bar of steel wei... ...might displace only about ...water, so it would sink. Thi... ...condition of negative buoy... ...volume and weight of a body ... ...volume and weight of the w... ...remains suspended in the liqu... ...as neutral buoyancy.

DIED

CRAWFORD — At the Greater Niagara General Hospital, on Wednesday, February 2, 1949, Nancy Ann Crawford, of 1939 Clark Street, in her 96th year, wife of the late John Crawford and aunt of Miss Stella Learn, Mrs. William Fero, Mrs. May Donald, Mrs. Ellman Learn and Jacob Learn all of this city, Mrs. Henry Laubacker, Mrs. Laura O'-Neil, Wesley Learn and Louis Peer of Niagara Falls, N.Y., and Mrs. Charles Newman of Stamford Township.

Resting at the Morse and Son Chapel, where services will be held on Saturday, February 5 at 2.00 p.m. Interment in Fairview Cemetery.
3

FUNERALS

MRS. NANCY A. CRAWFORD

Many lovely floral tributes banked the casket for the funeral services for Mrs. Nancy Ann Crawford, in the Morse and Son Chapel, on Saturday afternoon at two o'clock.

A host of friends and relatives attended the services which were conducted by Rev. Lorne Smith, minister of Main Street Baptist Church.

Interment was in Fairview Cemetery and the bearers were: Milbert Aikens, Ellman Learn, Jacob Learn, Louis Peer, Grant Haymes and Clayton Morningstar.

MRS. EVAN F. UPPER

LEARN — At the Greater Niagara General Hospital on Sunday, June 3, 1956, Lawrence Ellman Learn, in his 68th year, of 536 Welland Ave., dear brother of Mrs. William Fero (Nancy), Mrs. John Donald (Mae), Estelle Learn and Jacob Learn, all of this city and Wesley Learn of Niagara Falls, N.Y.

Resting at the Morse & Son Chapel where funeral service will be held on Tuesday, June 5th at 2 p.m. Interment Fairview Cemetery.

MRS. JOHN DONALD

Active lodge member

Mrs. John Robert Donald (Mae), 533 Welland Ave., who was active in fraternal circles, died Tuesday at the Greater Niagara General Hospital.

Born in Niagara Falls, she lived here all her life.

She was a member of St. Andrew's United Church.

She belonged to the Laura Secord Lodge, LOBA 161; the Blue Bell Rebekah Lodge 68; the Niagara Chapter 676 of the Women of the Moose.

She was also a member of the Rapids cribbage team and the Golden Hour Club.

Her husband, John Robert Donald, died in 1936.

One son John F. also predeceased her.

Surviving are one son, Gordon W., St. Catharines; one daughter, Mrs. Clayton Morningstar (Mildred), Niagara Falls; two sisters, Mrs. William Fero (Nancy) and Miss Estelle Learn, both of Niagara Falls; 11 grandchildren and 16 great grandchildren.

Mrs. Donald is at the Morse and Son Chapel where funeral service will be held Friday at 2 p.m.

Burial will be in Fairview cemetery.

OFFICE: HEWSON BLOCK, ERIE AVENUE.   TELEPHONE.

Niagara Falls, Ont. July 5th 1898.

Mr Geo Learn

Dr. to *Dr. Honsberger.*

		To a/c rendered	2 00
1891			
May	26	Mrs Pease Visit	1 00
	27	"	1 00
			4 00

Nancy Peer Crawford

Lydia written on back

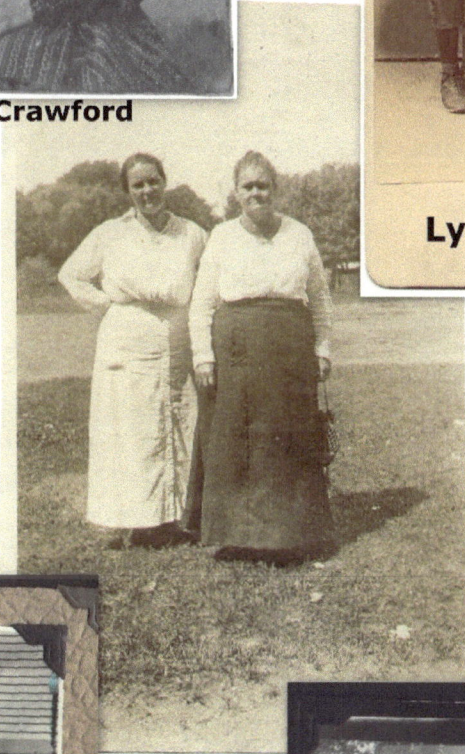

<---Maria Matilda Learn nee Peer & Mae

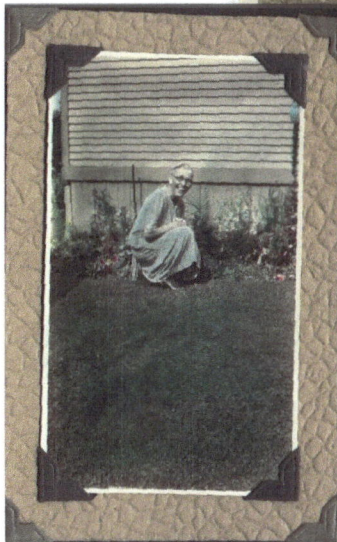

Nancy Peer Crawford bottom left & right

Lydia appears to be Lydia Peer, sister of Stephen Peer the Tightrope Walker

55

Stephen Peer son of Edward & Catherine 1840-1887

Tightrope walker died while on tightrope at Niagra Falls Ontario

Stephen Peer crossing Niagara River on a rope

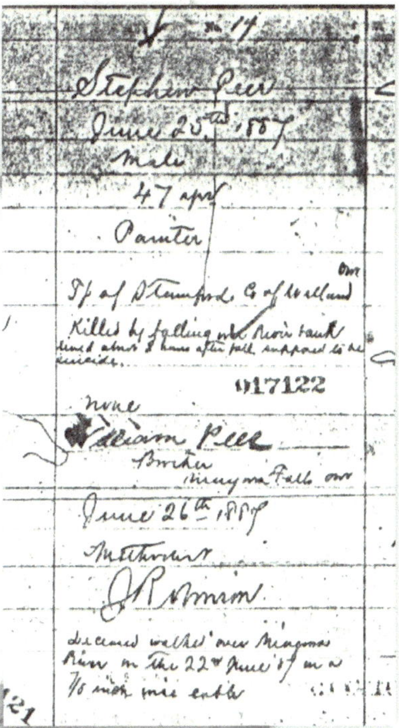

No 17

Stephen Peer

June 25th 1887

Male

47 yrs

Painter

Tp of Stamford Co of Welland Ont

Killed by falling near [illegible] tank lived about 2 hours after fall supposed to be suicide.

017122

none

William Peer
Brother
Niagara Falls Ont

June 26th 1887

Methodist

J Robinson

deceased walked over Niagara River on the 22nd June 87 on a 7/8 inch wire cable

EVENING REVIEW

EIGHTY YEARS OR MORE

STEPHEN PEER

With the eyes of the world centred on the Niagara River and the great ice drama which has been enacted during the past fortnight, we thought readers of this column would be interested in a sister's description of the feats of the late Stephen Peer, who would have been ninety-eight years if he had lived to see the collapse of the Falls View bridge. Three members of Peer's family are living. They are his sisters: Mrs. Nancy Crawford 84, Clark Avenue Mrs. Jane Caldwell 88, of Oakdale, Neb.; and a brother William Peer of Niagara Falls, N.Y., who is in his late seventies.

Stephen Peer was born at Montrose in 1840 and died at the age of forty-seven. His lifeless body was found on the cliff of the Niagara River about nine o'clock in the evening of June 25th, 1887, and his family always believed that he met with foul play. During the day preceding his death, Peer was seen in the company of two strange men. The trio walked to the bank of the river, near the point where Peer always started his tight-rope walks across the gorge. The two strangers stood talking for some time and when they turned around Peer had disappeared. Several hours later his body was found on the river bank, and his sister says there were marks about his throat which indicated violence.

The thrilling stunts of Blondin witnessed when he was a youngster, inspired young Peer to walk across the Niagara River on a tight rope and later on a small cable. He practised during his early years by twining wild grape vines into ropes which he strung among the trees in the orchard.

He learned the painter's trade, and while engaged in this work became accustomed to high places where a steady nerve was required. During the rope walking mania he became greatly fascinated with it and dreams of a princely fortune led him to try the feat.

When Balleni stepped into the limelight in 1873 with his stunts on the river, Peer assisted him in erecting his cable and did a bit of practising. Balleni refused to lend him his guide pole, so the local youth obtained a rail and it served the purpose. On one occasion Peer walked out on the rope and when the crowd cheered the young amateur, Balleni became so enraged he cut two strands of the rope, leaving one section between Peer and certain death if he plunged into the river. Balleni was nearly mobbed and had to move out of town. He left the rope strung across the river and never came back or sent for it.

Peer spent ten years of his life giving rope walking exhibitions and trapeze stunts over the river, and in American cities. "He made quite a good many trips across the river on the rope," Mrs. Crawford recounted yesterday. "I can remember the first day he tried it. I went down to the river. When Stephen started across I couldn't bear to look at him. Then I had to open my eyes, and I held my breath and hoped he would get across. He made the trip all right and after that I was never afraid."

On one occasion the crowd took up a collection for Peer and he put the money in his hat. On the return trip it was windy in the gorge and a gentle zephyr sent the cap spinning and Peer's money fell into the river.

In June 1887 Peer achieved his greatest success of his whole career when he walked across the gorge on a three-quarter inch wire cable—a mere thread compared with the rope that Blondin and others had used. It was considered more daring than that performed by any of his predecessors as the cable was smaller and fewer guys used. It was scheduled for May 24, but a heavy rain prevented Peer from making the trip. When the appointed day arrived in June, thousands of people gathered in the vicinity to witness the performance, new and novel to some and tame to others. Quite a heavy wind was blowing at the time appointed for the walk and it was feared that it would again be postponed, but Peer put in an appearance.

He was dressed in white tights, flesh colored shorts and red and black striped trunks. On his feet he wore tan-colored leather slippers like moccasins.

The wire cable was three-quarters of an inch in diameter and attached to it were twenty or thirty wire guys and between them a dozen to twenty sandbags weighing each about thirty-five pounds. The start was made from the Canadian shore, amid cheers of a very enthusiastic crowd. Peer moved slowly along until he reached the centre. Then he sat down and rested. After resting a few minutes he resumed his journey [illegible] twice in the last half of his trip, reaching the U. S. side amid the applause of the crowd on both banks of the river. He returned to Canada by the old suspension bridge in a carriage.

[illegible] an obituary notice it was said of Peer who was buried from the Main House: "He was a goodnatured man, and it is said that he had not an enemy in the world."

Tight-rope walker, library are discussed by historians

Factual information concerning the area was presented at the monthly meeting of The Lundy's Lane Historical Society held in the auditorium of the Drummond Branch Library.

Warren Adams and Mrs. Calvin Bessey gave papers on Stephen Peer, a local tight-rope walker, and the foundation of libraries in the Village of Drummondville and the Town of Clifton in the last century.

Mr. Adams pointed out that the first daredevil to cross the Niagara Gorge wasa native of France, Jean Francois de Gravelot whose professional name 'Blondin' is more familiar although more than 100 years have elapsed since his daring feats took place in 1859 and 1860.

Among the spectators who watched the great Blondin was a young man who lived in Stamford Township south of Lundy's Lane named Stephen Peer. The idea to cross the Niagara in imitation of Blondin's exploits dominated young Peer's life and on May 24, 1887, he demonstrated his ability publically in the Village of Drummondville by walking on a rope stretched from the Ellis Hotel, (the Prospect House) to Duncan's Store (Munroe and Zavitz Hardware Store.)

His years of preparation culminated in his life's ambition being realized on June 22, 1887, when in the presence of a great crowd gathered on the American as well as the Canadian banks of the river, he crossed the gorge on a wire, five eights of an inch in diameter.

Peer's walk across the gorge took place during the celebrations commemorating the golden anniversary of the ascension to the throne of England by Queen Victoria.

Three days later, on the night of June 25, Peer was missing. A search party was organized and his smashed body was discovered on the rocks of the gorge below the slender wire which a short time befor had carried him to fame. Sephen Peer's body lies interred in Fairview Cemetery.

[illegible] 1895 was changed to a public library under the provision of an act by the provincial legislature.

J. G. Robertson, tailor, whose place of business was situated at the corner of Culp and Main Streets provided a room and acted as librarian for an annual fee of $50. In 1898 additional room was required and Mr. Robertson's stipend was increased to $80.

Twenty years after the founding of the institute in Drummondville, a meeting inaugurating 'a Mechanics Institute and Reading room in the Town of Clifton, was held on October 3, 1878.

Located in the Howard block, later the Savoy Hotel at the corner of Bridge Street and Clifton Avenue, the institute opened its doors on January 2, 1879. The institute was moved to the town hall and to the Lundy block before the present library was built on Victoria Avenue in 1910.

In the meantime the library in Drummondville, (Niagara Falls South since the amalgamation in 1904), continued in rented premises until 1948 when the present building housing the Drummond Branch Library was opened.

Mrs. George W. Morse who sold the site for one half the commercial value of the property, was commended at that time for 'a valuable contribution of a private donor'.

The Stamford Centre Branch Library commenced operation in June, 1957, and was relocated in the Town and Country Plaza in 1962.

Mrs. Bessey indicated that the libraries of the City of Niagara Falls have grown from the foundation of the Drummondville and Mechanics Institute in 1858.

The institute was established by a group of public spirited citizens who also provided a collection of books for the reading room. Seven years later this nucleus of a library had expanded and the shelves now held 900 volumes. The institute carried on for 37 years and in

Stephen Peer of Townsend Township, Norfolk County

Named in *"Report of Persons recommended by Paul Averill, with the Lots subscribed for by them"* in Townsend Township, Norfolk County prepared by Acting Surveyor General David W. Smith dated on 5 Apr 1797 [Upper Canada Land Petitions "A" Bundle 3, Petition Number 62]

Grantee: Pier, Stephen W; authorized by Paul Averill on 9 Jan 1797; Oath of Allegiance sworn on 7 Jan [1797] by W. Dickson, Esq; Lot asked for: Lot 3 Concession 5

Receiver General's Office, York (Toronto) 18 April 1811

"Stephen Peer has paid into this Office three Pounds five Shillings & two pence Prov^l Currency the Pat. Fee on Lot N° 3 in the 5 Con of Townsend under Reg^s of 1796 & one Pound Seven Shillings & Six pence Curr^y the Survey^r Fees thereon. For the Recev^r Genl [Signature illegible]

Amount paid in £
3.5.2
1.7.6

——
4.12.8

Currency to John Small Esqr Clk of Executive Council"

Receiver Generals Office
York 18 April 1811

Stephen Peer has paid into the
Office Three Pounds, Five Shillings & two pence
Currency the Pat. Fee on Lot No 3 in the
Town of Townsend under Reg.n of 1796 & one
Pound, Seven Shillings & Six pence being the
Survey Fee thereon   For the Receiver Genl

£ 3 5 2
  1 7 6
  4 12 8 Currency

John Small Esqr
Clk. of Executive Council

Upper Canada Land Petitions, A Bundle 3, 1797-1799, RG1 L3, Vol. 2. Petition 62q. C-1609

The Skinner Family

Lydia Skinner was the daughter of Haggai Skinner and Elizabeth Westbrook. Haggai can be found at Niagara with a wife, 1 male child under 10, 1 male child over 10, 1 female child under 10 and 1 female child over 10 14 Nov. 1786 in Mr. Burches District [Niagara Falls]

11th April, 1797 - 25th April, 1797
Skinner, Benjamin, Junior - Praying for lands in addition to 200 acres which he has received. The petitioner having sold the land granted to him is not entitled to any further extension of His Majesty's bounty.

Skinner, Haggai - Praying for family lands. Ordered 100 acres for additional family lands.

About 1767, Haggai was living with his brother Daniel in Cochecton, New York and shared with him a business of rafting timber down the Delaware river to Philadelphia. He and Daniel were accused of having wounded several Indian chiefs at a party on Christmas Day, 1771 and potentially provoking a war, but were exonerated. Among those who testified to his and Daniel's good character were several named Westbrook.

In his petition of Feb 1797, Haggai stated that "in endeavouring to join the Royal Standard in the year 1778 was taken, and that he was kept in prison from that time until the conclusion of the war being upwards of four years." He came into the province in 1785 with a wife and five children, and now (1797) had 8 children. He had received 500 acres for himself and his family and was asking for 200 acres in addition " in consideration of his large family". He was recommended for 100 acres as family lands. Haggai was living in Stamford.

In 1810 he felt he had been treated unequally with other Loyalists, and on 15 January he petitioned the Governor that his name be added to the U.E. List: "That your petitioner came into the Province in the year 1785 near 400 miles through a wilderness with a wife and four children, and gratefully acknowledges to have received 650 acres of land on which he has paid the accustomed fees. -
Your petitioner having attached himself from the earliest stage of the American Revolution to the cause of his sovereign, assisted many others to enable them to join the Royal Standard and actually prepared himself to do the same in the year 1778 when he was unhappily enjoined upon and thrown into a loathsome prison, which imprisonment, after much suffering was exchanged to the Precinct in which he lived on giving ample security not to exceed its bounds during the war after which your petitioner lost no time in preparing to join the King's Standard and is now comfortably settled with a large family on the lands he has drawn.
Your petitioner seeing (not without some degree of mortification) others under similar circumstances and perhaps with less ---- on their side, whose families were

enjoying His Majesty's bounty as U.E. Loyalists whilst his family are all barred that priviledge, Humbly prays your Excellency will be pleased to --- that distinction by allowing the insertion of his name on the U.E. List."

Supporting his petition were Joel Westbrook of Pelham and Allan McDonald. Westbrook said that "he was well acquainted with Haggai Skinner in the time of the American Revolution, that he was much attached to the British and did aid and assist men to join the British standard, for so doing he was confined and kept prisoner till the year 1783". McDonald stated that Haggai "was taken prisoner in the year 1778 and kept a prisoner for four years thereby prevented joining the Royal Standard".

On June 19, 1810 he signed a petition on behalf of his daughter, Hulda, stating that "my name is inserted on the U E List to the best of my knowledge and belief".

During the War of 1812, in June 1813 when the Americans were occupying Niagara, Haggai Skinner 'Farmer, Falls, 64 years of age' was taken into custody with other non-combatants by order of Major General Dearborn. He was held for six months in the war prison at Greenbush and finally released on parole and sent to Fort George on 8 Dec 1813.

On 20 Sept 1815, Haggai submitted a claim for losses in the War of 1812 amounting to 186 Pounds. In Oct 1813 he lost to the American troops and Indians a number of personal items: a feather bed, four woollen blankets, a woollen coverlet, three linen sheets, 2 pillow cases, 30 yards of new linen, a great coat, a small coat, a pair of velvet pantaloons, 2 pair worsted stockings, a worsted belt, 2 cambric shirts, 3 muslim shirts, 1 calamanco petticoat, 2 calico gowns, 1 calico gown patnen, 3 pair woollen stockings and 2 handkerchiefs. On July 10 1814 (prior to the battle of Lundy Lane) he lost a horse, bridle and harness. To the British in Oct 1814 he lost 4 tons of hay, 1 acre of buckwheat, 500 bushels of apples, 16 bushels of potatoes and a saddle. Bills worth $125 were taken, and his house and barn were used for 5 weeks. He enclosed a receipt from Major Thomas Coates of the Light Dragoons dated 28 July 1814 for 400 weight of hay.

Claims for losses were not paid in 1815, and the claim was re-examined in 1823.

On 15 July 1817 he petitioned for the grant of 200 acres that he was entitled to as U.E. Loyalist, mentioning his imprisonment in two wars for his loyalty, and the fact that in 1810 his name was inserted on the U.E. List by Order in Council.

A reference to Haggai Skinner's death is the statement of Thomas Clark, a J.P. for Niagara District written on 4 March 1824 in support of the Claim for Losses in the War of 1812 by Job Skinner. [7] Clark wrote,

> From my knowledge of the late Job Skinner who when alive was my near
> neighbour and resided on the public road, opposite the Falls - I believe that

he must have lost considerably during the late war, his farm being contiguous to the scene of action at Lundy Lane in 1814 - his father Timothy Skinner who resided with him died during the war, himself dying shortly afterward and his uncle and neighbour Haggai Skinner having died last autumn, makes it difficult to get more particular proof of his claim at so distant a period . .

Stephen Peer's name is found in the will of Timothy Skinner. [Lincoln County Wills #2198; filed 25 Sept 1815; Ontario Archives Reel GS1-649]

"In the name of god Amen. I Timothy Skinner Senior of the majestic Province of Upper Canada District of Niagara County of Lincoln & Township of Stamford being weak of body but of sound and perfect mind and Memory blessed be almighty god for the same do this Eleventh day of may one Thousand Eight Hundred and Seven make constitute and publish this my last Will and Testament (that is to say) Imprimus(?). I commend my soul into the Hand and protection of almighty god, who gave it to me and my body to the earth to be buried in a Christian like manner in hopes of a Joyful Resurrection through the merits of my Saviour Jesus Christ, and as for that worldly Estate wherewith it hath pleased god to bless me, I dispose thereof as follows First I give and bequesth unto my beloved wife Patience Skinner one third part of the Real profits of my land and tenements during her widowhood Together with one third part of my Moveable property an personal Estate. To my oldest Son Isaiah Skinner I give and bequest twenty one shillings. I also give and bequesth to my second son Henry Skinner twenty one shillings. I also give and bequesth to my third son Aaron Skinner twenty one Shillings. I also give and bequesth to my fourth Son Timothy Skinner Junior Twenty one Shillings. I also give and bequesth to my fifty Son Job Skinner the whole of the farm in wherein I now dwell to him and the male heirs of his body lawfully begotten for ever and Ever together with nine acres of land adjoining. To him and his heirs for ever. which said nine acres I purchased of my Fourth Son Timothy Skinner Junior and I likewise give and bequesth unto my fifth Son Job Skinner all the Remaining Moisly (?) or two thirds of my moveable property or personal Estate. I also give and bequesth unto my two oldest daughters that is to say Mary Quivey and Rhoda Terry two hundred acres of land that is to say lot Number Eighteen in the Twelfth Concession of Blenheim (I being possessed of no better description of said land at present) Share and Share alike to them the said Mary Quivey and Rhoda Terry and the male hirs of their and each of their bodies for ever. I also give and bequeath to my third daughter Sarah Haun one hundred acres of land that is to say the northernmost Fifty acres of lot Number Eleven in the Sixth concession of Blenheim and Fifty of lot number three in Fourteenth Concession of Pelham Township to her and the male heirs of her body for ever. I also give and bequeath to my fourth and Fifth daughers Lois and Patience Skinner Two hundred acres of Land viz. Lot number Nineteen in the Twelfth Concession of Blenheim Township to them and the male heirs of their and Their bodies for ever Share and Share alike. I also give and bequeath to my Grandson Collin Skinner one hundred acres of land viz the East end of lot Number Fourteen in the County of York Township of York and Second Concession to him and the male heirs of his body

lawfully begotten for Ever as I have bequesthed my estate in Blenhiem Township without mentioning the County I declare that I have forgot what county it is in. With respect to Funeral Charges and other debts wherein I do, or many Stand indebted at my decease it is my will that they be paid out of my moveable Property and the farm whereon I now dwell and I do hereby make ordain Constitute and appoint my Brother Haggia Skinner Senior Noah Cook and my Fifth Son Job Skinner may be my true and lawful executors to this my last will hereby revoking all former wills by me made. In witness whereof I have hereunto set my hand and Seal the day and year first above written. --- Signed Sealed Published and declared by the above named Timothy Skinner Senior to be his last will and Testament. In the prescence of us and each of us who have hereunto subscribed our name as witnesses in the presence of the Testator.
(signed)
Hamilton Graham
Timothy Skinner Senior
Stephen Peer
John Misener

To His Excellency the Governor in Council of Upper Canada &c.
The petition of the Subscribers (Inhabitants of Lincoln County Stamford Township) - - Most respectfully sheweth that there is great want of Mills at or near the Falls of Niagara . We therefore pray that Timothy Skinner (Senior) may be tolerated to build said mills adjoining his own land and as in duty bound we shall ever pray.
(signed)

Thomas Millard	*Azariah Lundy*
Chas Willson	*William Lundy*
James Forsyth	*Jacob Fonger*
Haggai Skinner	*William Fonger*
Noah Cook	*Charles Grene*
John Harvey	*Benjamin Skinner Senior*
Edwd Lafferty	*Ebenezir Skinner*
John Losca	*Isaac Chambers*
John Durham	*Robert Spencer his X mark*
Edward Durham	*James Crawford*
Thomas Millard Junior	*Chris Bulmer (?)*
John Reilly	*Henry Ramsey*
Peter McMicking	*James Goball (?)*
Jacob Kilman	*Thomas Doan*
John McKinlie(?)	*John Upper*
John Clow	*Jacob Upper*
Adam McNair	*George Upper*
Peter Thomson	*George Couke*
Paul Cripps	*Robert Wilkerson*
Archibald Thomson	*Benajah (?) Williams*
John Thomson	*George Keefer*
Thomas McMicking	*John Rily (?)*
Joseph Robeson his mark X	*Ezekial Woodruff*

John Chisholm
Donald Ross
James Cooper
Conrad Darshimer (?)
Patrick Reilly
Benjamin Skinner

Giles Hall
Hugh Wilson
John Wilson
John Wilson Junr
John Silverthorn

To His Honor Peter Rusell Esquire
administering the Government of Upper Canada
&c &c &c   In Council —

The Petition of Haggai Skinner
of Bamford

Humbly sheweth

That your Petitioner is a
Loyalist, and came to this Province in the year
1785 with a wife and 5 Children, having now 8
— that he has received 200 acres for himself
& 300 acres as family Lands — for which he is
very thankful — That your Petitioner in
endeavouring to join the Royal Standard in
the year 1778 was taken, and that he
was kept in Prison from that time to the
conclusion of the war being upwards
of four years — Your Petitioner therefore
humbly hopes, that in consideration of
his large family, as well as for considerable
of his Loyalty, your Honor would be pleased to
grant him 200 acres in addition to the Land he has
received and your Petitioner as in duty bound will
ever pray —

this petition was personally
applied for by Haggai Skinner
T.R.D.q.U.

Bamford
Feb. 1797

1390

No 179 No 46
Royal River
Rec.d 10 March 1797
Rec.d 2.d May
Order in Council
a recommends

act 17 May 99

139

These are to Certify that the Bearer Haggiah Skinner. that I have — Been fully Acquainted with him and his family Ever Since the year 1775 and he always Shewed himself a true and loyal Subject to his Majesty and in the year 1795 in the — Month of July Came in to this province and Remaind as a litter Ever Since and in with him — brout A wife and five Children

Alexr Donald

138c

I do hereby Certify that Haggai Skinner
Came into this province in the Year 1785,
that he has made a Large Improvement
that he has been Always Considered as an honest &
Very Industrious man, that he has one child
born in this province before the Year 1789 —

Given under my hand at Stamford
this 27th April 1797 –

John Reilly J.P.

Isaac Swayze J.P.

103

To His Excellency Francis Gore Esquire Lieutenant
Governor of the Province of Upper Canada &c
&c &c in Council

The Petition of Maggee Skinner of the
Township of Clanford

Humbly Sheweth

That your Petitioner came into the
Province in the Year 1785, near 400 Miles
through a Wilderness with a wife and
four Children, and gratefully acknowledges to have received 650 Acres of Land
on which he has paid the accustomed
fees. —

Your Petitioner having attach'd
himself from the earliest stage of the
American Revolution to the cause
of his Sovereign, assisted many others
to enable them to Join the Royal Standard
and actually prepared himself to do the
same in the Year 1778 when he was
unhappily informed upon and thrown
into a Loathsome Prison, which imprisonment after much suffering was enlarged
to the Precinct in which he lived on giving
ample security not to exceed its bounds
during the war, after which your
Petitioner

103a

Petitioner lost no time in preparing to
Join the King's Standard and is now com-
-fortably settled with a large Family on the
Lands he has drawn.

Your Petitioner seeing (not without some
degree of Mortification) others under similar
circumstances, and perhaps with less Losses
on their Side, whose Families are enjoying
His Majesty's bounty to U.E. Loyalists whilst
his Family are deprived that privilege
Humbly prays your Excellency will be pleased
to remove that distinction by allowing him
the insertion of his Name on the U.E. List

and your Petitioner as in duty bound
will ever pray &c &c &c

Stamford January 15th 1810.

Haggai Skinner

I Solemnly and Sincerely Swear that
what I have inserted in the above petition
is the Truth & help me god

Sworn before in
Willoughby Jany 15th   Haggai Skinner
          1810

Sam'l Street J.P.

103b

I certify that the Petitioner Ragner Skinner
came into the Province in the year 1785 with
a Wife and Family, and by his frugality
Sobriety and Industry is now one of our
best Farmers — what he has shewn,
or further set forth in his Petition I
believe to be the truth —

Willoughby Janry 15th 1808

Saml Steel JP

103

Joel Westbrook maketh Oath and Say. that he
Was well acquainted With Maggai Skinner in the time
of the American Revolution that he Was much attach'd
to the British and Listed and Enlist Men to Join
the British Standard for Joining he Was confined
and Kept prisoner till the Year 1783

Sworn before the
at Pelham the 8th Janu 1810

Joel Westbrook

Amos Chapman J.P.

103

Personally came before me Alex Wood
Esqr. One of his Majestys Justices of the
Peace for the Home District. Allan
McDonell of the Township of Gainsborough
in the District of Niagara who made oath
on the Holy Evangelists that he is personally acquainted with Haggarah Skinner
of the Township of Stamford & that he was
taken prisoner in the year 1778 and kept
a prisoner for some years & thereby prevented joining the Royal Standard.
Sworn before me at
York the 20th Feby 1810   Allan McDonald

Alexander Wood JP

Endnotes

[1] Upper Canada Land Petitions. C-2490. P10/11

[2] RG 5 A1, Vol 20, pp 8600-8602, National Archives of Canada reel C-4544. Also Upper Canada Sundries V. 23 PAGE p. 10119

[3] RED COATS AND GREY JACKETS by Donald E. Granes

[4] The Niagara Portage Road" by Ernest Green in Ontario Historical Society Papers & Records, Vol. XXIII, 1926 p. 310

[5] War of 1812 list of orphans, Pensioners and Widows published in the Kingston Gazette, Kingston, Upper Canada, Sat. 4 Jan, 1817 in Families Vol. 31 #3 Aug. 1992

[6] compiled by Douglas A. Robbins, Early Marriages in the Niagara Peninsula, 1818 Sep. 6. John Barker, bachelor, and Lydia Pier (Stamford).

[7] Upper Canada: War of 1812 Losses Claims, RG 19 E 5(a), Vol 3751, No. 1028. National Archives. <http://freepages.genealogy.rootsweb.com/~russmcgillivray/skinner/page1.html#27>